Success guides

Standard Grade
Home Economics

Edna Hepburn ✗ Jean McAllister

Contents

Exam technique 4

Eating a variety of foods contributes to good health

Nutrients 1 8
Nutrients 2 10
Nutrients 3 12
Health, water and dietary fibre (NSP) 13
Health and nutrient intake 14
Test your progress 16

Current dietary advice in relation to good health

Current dietary advice 1 18
Current dietary advice 2 20
Diet and health 22
Food labelling 25
Test your progress 26

Individuals have varying dietary needs

Dietary requirements 1 28
Dietary requirements 2 30
Dietary requirements 3 32
Factors affecting food choice 33
Test your progress 34

Cleanliness is important in relation to health

Hygiene 36
Food spoilage 38
Preserving food 41
Controlling bacterial growth 42
Food storage in the home 44
Test your progress 46

Safe practices are important in the use of resources and procedures

Current safe practices 1   48
Current safe practices 2   50
Safety around the home   52
Test your progress   54

Design features are an important consideration in the choice of materials and equipment

Influences on choice of materials and equipment   56
Design areas   58
Conservation of resources   60
Test your progress   62

Individuals and families have different physical needs

Clothing 1   64
Clothing 2   66
Shelter   68
Well-being   69
Consumer advice 1   70
Consumer advice 2   72
Test your progress   74

Management of personal and household expenditure

Income and budgeting   76
Essential and non-essential expenditure   78
Purchasing goods   80
Debt management   82
Test your progress   84

Exam-style questions and answers   86
Index   96

How to answer exam questions

The Standard Grade Home Economics exam assesses **Knowledge and Understanding** (KU) and **Handling Information** (HI) at Foundation, General and Credit levels. Read carefully the following information on how to answer the different types of exam questions.

Knowledge and Understanding

These questions are about what you **know** and what you **learned** throughout your course.

You may find the following words and phrases in KU exam questions:

- choose
- explain
- give **one** reason
- give a **different** reason
- identify and explain
- explain in detail.

If **one mark** is to be awarded then give **one answer**.

If **one question** is worth **2 marks**, you must make sure you give **extra detail** in your answer.

To make sure you gain full marks in KU questions:

- check your answer links to the **key words** of the question
- then ask yourself 'why?' or 'how?' or 'so?' – if you can answer this, then write it down.

For writing the **extra detail** you will gain an **extra mark**.

Top Tip

Whether the question is KU or HI, you should:
- start by **reading** the question **carefully**
- **underline** or **highlight** the **key words** of the question
- look at the **marks** being awarded for each question, as this will tell you how many answers to give.

Applying exam technique to KU questions

Start by highlighting the key words.

General level

A café is preparing healthy beefburgers. Study the ingredients below.

- wholemeal bread
- lean minced beef
- carrot
- onion
- garlic
- mixed herbs

Choose **three** ingredients from the list and identify which Scottish dietary target each helps to meet. [3]

Explain why **each** choice benefits health. [6]

Answers and marks

		Marks awarded
Ingredient 1	*Wholemeal bread*	
Scottish dietary target	*Bread intake to increase, mainly using wholemeal*	1
Benefit to health	*It contains non-starch polysaccharides (NSP)*	1
	+ which helps to prevent constipation	+ 1
Ingredient 2	*Lean minced beef*	
Scottish dietary target	*Eat less fat*	1
Benefit to health	*It is low in fat*	1
	+ which helps to prevent heart disease	+ 1
Ingredient 3	*Carrot*	
Scottish dietary target	*Eat more fruit and vegetables*	1
Benefit to health	*They are low in sugar*	1
	+ which helps prevent obesity	+ 1

Full marks have been awarded for this answer. Why?

Look at the marks awarded at the right-hand side (**3 marks** for **each** complete answer):

- 1 mark has been awarded for **each** correct dietary target
- 1 mark has been awarded for **why** each food links to the dietary target
- 1 mark has been awarded for **how** each dietary target benefits health.

All answers **link** to the highlighted key words.

CREDIT

Credit level

Explain **two** benefits to health of eating oily fish. **[4]**

Answers and marks

		Marks awarded
Benefit 1	*It contains vitamin D*	1
	+ which helps the absorption of calcium to prevent rickets	+ 1
Benefit 2	*Oily fish contain omega 3 fatty acids*	1
	+ which help reduce the risk of heart disease	+ 1

Full marks have been awarded for this question. Why?

Look at the marks being awarded at the right-hand side (**2 marks** for **each** complete answer):

- 1 mark has been awarded for **each** correct nutrient in oily fish
- 1 mark has been awarded for **how** each nutrient benefits health.

All answers **link** to the highlighted key words.

Top Tip
Remember: to know the **benefits to health** of **any food**, you must know about **nutrients** and **dietary diseases**.

Handling information

These questions will usually **give** you the information you require to answer the question.

This information will be in the form of a case study and chart of information.

You may find the following words in HI exam questions:

- choose and give reasons
- choose the most suitable
- give reasons/detailed reasons
- give different reasons
- evaluate the suitability.

Sometimes you have to select the **most suitable item** for the situation and you will be awarded one mark.

If **one mark** is to be awarded then give **one answer**.

If **one question** is worth **two marks**, you must make sure you give **extra detail** in your answer or you will not gain an extra mark.

In some evaluation questions, no best choice is asked for and you are expected to **evaluate** one or more items.

To make sure you gain full marks in HI questions:

- you must **link** the information in the **chart** to the **case study** *and also*
- give reasons **why** that link is important to the given situation in the case study.
- To **evaluate**, think about why the item is **suitable** or **unsuitable**, **good** or **bad**.
- Use the words **so**, **therefore**, **because** or **as** to help you evaluate.
- Some evaluation answers need to explain the **consequences** of the choice.

Applying exam technique to HI questions

General level

Mr and Mrs Brown work full time and have three teenage children. All the family take part in a number of sporting activities. All existing electric sockets are used by other appliances as the kitchen is small. They own a microwave cooker and a dishwasher. Because they are interested in cooking healthy meals, they are planning to buy a steamer.

Look at the following information about steamers.

Steamer A	**Steamer B**	**Steamer C**
Holds 4 servings	Holds 2 servings	Holds 6 servings
Two large steam baskets	One steam basket	Three large steam baskets
Electric steamer	Use in a saucepan	Use in microwave
Not dishwasher proof	Not dishwasher proof	Dishwasher proof
Fast or slow cooking option	Cooking time varies with food	Food can be cooked quickly

Choose the **most suitable** steamer for this family. [1]

Give **two** reasons for your choice. [4]

Answers and marks	*Marks awarded*

Most suitable choice: *Steamer C* — 1

Reason 1 *This steamer is dishwasher proof* — 1
+ which is a good choice because they have a dishwasher so it would save them time washing up — +1

Reason 2 *It has 3 large baskets/holds 6 servings and there are 5 people in the Brown family* — 1
+ who will need a large amount of food to be cooked at once — +1

Full marks have been awarded for this question.

All answers **link** to the key words and the **information in the chart**.
Steamer C is judged to be most suitable to the needs of the Brown family.

Credit level

CREDIT

In DRV evaluation questions, marks will be awarded like this:
- 1 mark for **evaluating the suitability** of the nutrient or energy intake
- 1 mark for **explaining the importance** of the nutrient or energy intake linked to the situation/case study
- 1 mark for **stating the consequence** to the situation/case study.

Taking account of the Dietary Reference Values for females aged 15–18 years old, **evaluate the suitability** of the day's meals for a 16 year old female who spends a lot of her leisure time taking part in activities at the sports centre and competing for the school's swimming club. **[9]**

Dietary Reference Values for Females aged 15–18 (per day)

Est Average Requirement	Reference Nutrient Intakes				
Energy	Protein	Iron	Calcium	Vitamin C	Sodium
8.83 MJ	45g	14.8mg	800mg	40mg	1600mg

Dietary analysis of the whole day's meals

Energy	Protein	Iron	Calcium	Vitamin C	Sodium
9.75 MJ	56.1g	8.3mg	820mg	25mg	2300mg

Answers and marks	*Marks awarded*

1 *The iron intake is not good as it is lower than the RNI.* — 1
Iron is important for making haemoglobin which carries oxygen in the blood to body tissues. — 1
+ As the girl is active she may become more easily tired and listless. — +1

2 *The meals are higher in protein than the RNI for the 16 year old girl which may be good.* — 1
Protein is needed for growth, repair and maintenance of body cells. — 1
+ The girl could injure herself when taking part in activities so this may help repair her injuries. — +1

3 *Vitamin C is lower than the RNI. This is not good because Vitamin C is needed to help the absorption of iron and the iron is also below the RNI so the girl may become anaemic.* — 1
— +2

Full marks have been awarded for this question.

All answers **link** to the key words and the **information in the DRV chart**.

Nutrients 1

It is important for good health to eat a balanced diet. A balanced diet provides all the necessary **nutrients** in the right amount to meet an individual's needs. One way to follow a balanced diet is to make sure we eat a variety of foods which supply a range of nutrients. Each nutrient has a specific function (or use) within the body.

There are **5 main nutrients** that you need to study: **proteins**, **carbohydrates**, **fats**, **vitamins** and **minerals**.

Top Tip
You must know the main food sources of a nutrient because you may be asked to identify nutrients found in a specific meal or food.

Protein

Functions:

- For **growth** of body tissues/cells in children.
- For **repair** of body tissues/cells in children and adults.
- For **maintenance** of body tissues.
- Excess protein can be used as a **source of energy**.

Proteins are made up of **amino acids**. Our bodies can make some of these amino acids but not all. We obtain those which our bodies cannot make from the food we eat. These are called **essential amino acids**.

CREDIT

These are called **high biological value (HBV) proteins**. These foods contain all eight essential amino acids required for growth, repair and maintenance of cells and tissues.

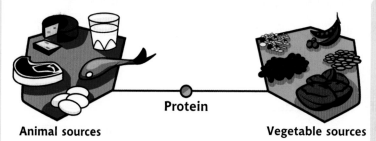

Protein

Animal sources　　　　**Vegetable sources**

These are called **low biological value (LBV) proteins**. These foods tend to lack one or more of the essential amino acids. One vegetable source contains all the essential amino acids – soya beans.

Carbohydrates

Functions:

- Provide energy for all activities; all activities use energy supplied by food.
- Provide warmth – excess carbohydrates can be converted into body fat and provide warmth.

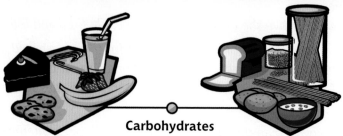

Carbohydrates

Sugars
Refined sugar, products containing refined sugar, e.g. sweets, cakes, biscuits, soft drinks, fruit

Starches (or Total Complex Carbohydrates, TCC)
Cereals e.g. oats, rice, cereal foods, e.g. bread, pasta, breakfast cereals, vegetables, e.g. potatoes, lentils

Carbohydrates can be divided into three main groups:

CREDIT

Group	Types	Sources
Monosaccharides	glucose	fruits
	fructose	fruit, vegetables, honey
	galactose	milk
Disaccharides	sucrose	sugar cane, beet (all products using these)
	maltose	produced during the fermentation of grain
	lactose	milk
Polysaccharides	starch	bread, breakfast cereals, potatoes, pasta, rice
	NSP	wholegrain products, e.g. wholemeal bread, fruit and vegetables

Top Tip
When you are revising for your exam eat plenty of starchy carbohydrates. These foods release energy slowly, helping you concentrate, and are filling.

Fats

Top Tip
Omega 3, found in oily fish, may improve your learning power.

Functions:

- Provide a very concentrated source of energy.
- Provide warmth – excess fats (those not used to supply energy) are converted to body fat and stored under the skin providing an insulating layer.
- Provide a source of fat soluble vitamins A, D, E and K.
- Provide essential fatty acids, especially omega 3. *CREDIT*

Saturated fats

Food sources: butter, cream, lard, meat, cheese, milk and many baked foods. If eaten in excess, saturated fats are considered bad for health as they may cause obesity and heart disease.

Fats

Unsaturated fats

Food sources: vegetable oils, e.g. sunflower or corn oil, polyunsaturated margarine

Health check on fats

Unsaturated fats are better for health as there is less risk of heart disease.

Essential fatty acids are found in unsaturated fats such as vegetable oils and oily fish such as salmon, sardines. Omega 3 is an important essential fatty acid as it reduces the risk of blood clots forming and so lessens the risk of heart disease and strokes. *CREDIT*

Quick Test

Top Tip
Usually you are not asked for more than two functions of a particular nutrient.

1. How can you ensure your diet is balanced?
2. Name the five main nutrients.
3. Name two sources of animal protein and two sources of vegetable protein.
4. What are the two main types of carbohydrates?
5. Which vitamins can be found in fatty foods?

Answers 1. By eating a variety of foods to ensure a range of nutrients. **2.** Proteins, carbohydrates, fats, vitamins and minerals. **3.** Animal – meat, fish, cheese, eggs or milk; vegetable – peas, beans, lentils, nuts, cereals, soya beans. **4.** Sugars and starches. **5.** Vitamins A, D, E and K.

Nutrients 2

Vitamins are very important to good health but are required in very small quantities. Vitamins can be described as being soluble in either **fat** or **water**.

Fat soluble vitamins

Vitamin A

Functions	Sources
• Growth in children • Necessary for good eyesight, particularly in dim light. • Protects skin tissues, e.g. lining of nose, mouth, throat and eyes. • Classed as an antioxidant, it can help reduce the risk of heart disease and cancers.	• Liver, butter, margarine, meat, cheese, eggs, oily fish. • Carrots, spinach, green vegetables, orange and red coloured fruit and vegetables.

Top Tip
Liver is a very rich source of vitamin A. Pregnant women should not eat it because it could be harmful for the developing baby.

Vitamin D

Functions	Sources
• Works with calcium and phosphorus to develop strong bones and teeth. • Helps absorption of calcium. • Helps bone fractures to heal quicker. • Prevents rickets in children (soft leg bones which bend).	• Sunlight. • Oily fish, egg yolk, liver, margarine. • Fortified breakfast cereals.

Top Tip
A variety of food products can be fortified. This means that additional nutrients have been added to improve the nutritional content.

Vitamin E

Functions	Sources
• Classed as an antioxidant vitamin. It can help reduce the risk of heart disease and cancers. • Maintains cell membranes.	• Vegetable oils, margarine, green leafy vegetables, cereal products, rice, oats. • Eggs.

Vitamin K

Functions	Sources
• Required for the clotting of blood.	• Milk, eggs. • Green leafy vegetables.

CREDIT

Water soluble vitamins

Vitamin B group

There are a number of different B vitamins in this group but they do have some functions in common.

General functions	Sources
• Release energy from foods. • Required for normal growth in children.	• Pork, bacon, liver, kidney, dairy foods. • Unprocessed whole foods, e.g. wholemeal flour and cereals, bread, yeast, potatoes.

Vitamin B1

Functions	Sources
• Releases energy from carbohydrates. • Helps with the functioning of the nervous system.	• Milk, meat, liver, eggs. • Flour, bread, fortified breakfast cereals, cereals.

CREDIT

Vitamin B2

Functions	Sources
• Releases energy from protein, carbohydrates and fats. • Essential for normal growth in children.	• Meat, liver, kidney, milk, eggs. • Green vegetables, wholemeal bread, yeast.

Folic acid

Functions	Sources
• Needed for the formation of red blood cells. • Helps protect against neural tube defects such as spina bifida in unborn babies.	• Liver, kidney. • Dark green leafy vegetables, wholegrain cereals and breads, fortified breakfast cereals, pulses.

Top Tip
Although pregnant women should take in extra folic acid, they should not obtain it from liver, as this is too rich a source of vitamin A, which can be harmful for the developing baby.

Vitamin C

Functions	Sources
• Helps the absorption of iron and so helps prevent anaemia. • Helps in the formation of connective tissue which holds body cells together. • Helps prevent infections. • Helps cuts and wounds to heal quicker.	• Citrus fruits (oranges, lemons, limes, grapefruit), kiwi fruit, strawberries, blackcurrants, green vegetables, peppers, cabbage, potatoes.

• Is one of the antioxidant vitamins that helps to reduce the risk of heart disease and cancers. *CREDIT*

Quick Test

1. Name the two groups of vitamins.

2. Which vitamin helps you to see in dim light?

3. Name two sources of folic acid.

4. Which vitamin helps wounds to heal more quickly?

Answers 1. Fat soluble and water soluble. 2. Vitamin A. 3. Liver, kidney, dark green leafy vegetables, wholegrain cereals, wholegrain bread, pulses, fortified breakfast cereals. 4. Vitamin C.

Nutrients 3

Iron

Functions	Sources
• Required for red blood cell formation. • Red blood cells (haemoglobin) carry oxygen round the body. • Prevents anaemia.	• Red meat, especially kidneys, liver, corned beef. • Fortified flour, bread, breakfast cereals, green leafy vegetables.

Calcium

Functions	Sources
• Needed for growth and development of bones and teeth, preventing rickets in children. • Helps in the normal clotting of blood. • Required for the normal functioning of muscles and nerves. • Combines with phosphorus to give calcium phosphate.	• Tinned fish with bones that can be eaten, e.g. salmon, sardines. • Milk, cheese, yoghurt. • Flour, fortified white bread. 

Fluoride

Functions	Sources
• Essential for the hardening of the enamel of teeth. • Helps to ensure that bones have the correct amounts of minerals deposited in them.	• Drinking water if it has been fluoridated. • Small quantities found in tea and saltwater fish. • Fluoride toothpaste.

Sodium

Functions	Sources
• Needed to maintain the correct concentration of body fluids. • Required for correct muscle and nerve activity – too low an intake can result in muscle cramps.	• Bacon, cheese. • Salt. • Convenience foods, savoury snacks, e.g. crisps.

Note: excess sodium can be linked to high blood pressure.

Phosphorus

Functions	Sources
• Works with calcium to give strength to bones and teeth.	• Milk and milk products, meat and meat products, fish.

Health, water and dietary fibre (NSP)

Water

Functions

- It is required for all our body fluids (e.g. blood, urine).
- It helps in the removal of waste products from all our body tissues and organs.
- Nearly all our body processes need water for them to take place, e.g. digestion, absorption of nutrients.
- It also helps to regulate body temperature.

Sources

Nearly 65% of the body is water. To maintain our body fluid levels we need to drink at least eight drinks (water, fruit juice, tea, coffee, diluted drinks) every day. Most foods contain water – fruit and vegetables consist mainly of water.

There are times when it is even more important to drink water:

- during exercise
- during illness – fever, vomiting, diarrhoea
- in hot weather
- during lactation when milk is being produced for breast feeding.

Top Tip
You need to drink plenty of water, particularly when studying and preparing for exams, as it helps the brain to function well.

Dietary fibre (NSP)

Top Tip
In an exam, if you are asked about nutrients, remember that water and NSP are not nutrients.

Functions

- It is needed for the digestive system to function properly. NSP (non starch polysaccharide) absorbs water and binds with other foods to make the faeces soft and bulky to help removal from the body.
- A diet rich in dietary fibre can help prevent constipation, bowel diseases such as diverticular disease, haemorrhoids (piles) and cancer of the colon.
- It can help give a feeling of fullness, which may prevent snacking; as part of a calorie-controlled diet this may be useful in preventing obesity.
- A good intake of dietary fibre will also help the removal of cholesterol from the body.

Sources

- Wholegrain cereals such as oats, wheat, rice, wholemeal bread.
- Fruit (with skins on) and vegetables, particularly leafy vegetables.

Quick Test

1. Which two foods consist mostly of water?
2. List two sources of NSP.
3. How can NSP help to prevent heart disease?

Answers 1. Fruit and vegetables. **2.** Wholegrain cereals, e.g. oats, wheat, rice, wholemeal bread, fruit, vegetables. **3.** By helping to remove cholesterol from the body; by preventing obesity.

Health and nutrient intake

The interrelationships between health, energy and protein are important to good health.

Health and energy

When you eat fat, carbohydrate and protein foods, energy is released to allow the body to carry out all its normal activities. **It is important that the amount of energy from food you eat is equal to the amount of energy your body requires for your activities.**

If you eat more food than you require, the excess energy from the food will be stored as fat, resulting in weight gain.

If you do not eat enough food to meet your energy needs, you will become tired and lacking in energy.

Health and protein

Protein is required for growth, repair and maintenance of body cells and tissues.

If too much protein is eaten, the excess is converted to fat and stored in the body, resulting in weight gain.

If insufficient protein is eaten then the body cannot carry out the normal function of growth and repair.

On page 8 you looked at HBV and LBV protein foods. HBV proteins contain all the 8 essential amino acids. LBV proteins are missing one or more of these essential amino acids. However, if a variety of LBV foods are eaten together, then the essential amino acids missing from one food can be found in another food. In other words, these foods **complement** each other.

The multi-nutrient value of food

Top Tip
Choose another food, e.g. vegetable lasagne, and map out all the nutrients.

Most foods contain **more than one nutrient**. No single food provides all the nutrients so it is very important to eat a balanced diet to obtain a variety of nutrients. The example here shows how many nutrients you can obtain from a tuna pizza.

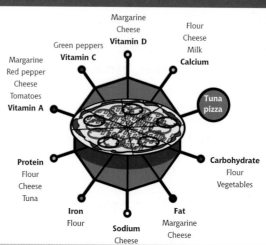

Margarine
Cheese
Vitamin D

Flour
Cheese
Milk
Calcium

Green peppers
Vitamin C

Margarine
Red pepper
Cheese
Tomatoes
Vitamin A

Tuna
pizza

Carbohydrate
Flour
Vegetables

Protein
Flour
Cheese
Tuna

Iron
Flour

Sodium
Cheese

Fat
Margarine
Cheese

Interrelationship of nutrients

Our bodies need a large amount of nutrients to maintain good health. Nutrients have specific functions but many work **together** and they have an important role to play **together**.

Calcium, phosphorus and vitamin D

- These three nutrients work **together** to help build and maintain strong bones and teeth.
- Calcium combines with phosphorus to make calcium phosphate, which is the material that gives hardness and strength to bones and teeth. **Both** calcium **and** phosphorus are needed for this process. Vitamin D is required for the absorption of these minerals.
- The absorption of calcium and phosphorus is controlled by vitamin D. If there is insufficient vitamin D in the diet, less calcium will be available to form strong bones and teeth.

Iron and vitamin C

- Vitamin C assists with the absorption of iron by changing it into a form that is more easily absorbed in the body. It is important to include vitamin C foods in the diet.
- Absorption of iron can be **hindered** by NSP and phytic acid.
- Absorption of calcium can be **hindered** by phytic acid, NSP, fats and oxalic acid.
- Absorption of calcium can be **assisted** by vitamin D, protein and lactose.

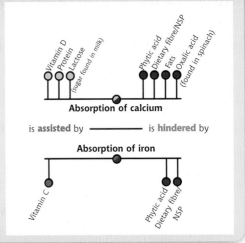

Quick Test

1. Using the ingredients in the tuna pizza, complete a chart to show the nutrients contained in each ingredient. Example: **Ingredient:** flour
   Nutrients: protein, calcium, iron, carbohydrates

2. State two factors which assist the absorption of calcium.

3. How does vitamin C help iron to be absorbed in the body?

4. Which vitamin controls the absorption of calcium and phosphorus?

5. What is the name of the substance that gives hardness to teeth and bones?

Answers 1. flour: protein, calcium, iron, carbohydrates; cheese: protein, fat, vitamin A, vitamin D; calcium, sodium; tuna: protein; margarine: fat, vitamin A, vitamin D: red pepper: vitamin A, carbohydrates; green pepper: carbohydrates, vitamin C; tomatoes: carbohydrates, vitamin A. **2.** Vitamin D, protein, lactose. **3.** By changing it into a form that is more easily absorbed in the body. **4.** Vitamin D. **5.** Calcium phosphate.

Test your progress

Use the questions to test your progress.

1. What is a balanced diet?
....

2. Explain two functions of protein in the diet.
....

3. State one function of carbohydrate in the body.
....

4. Give three sources of total complex carbohydrate in the diet.
....

5. State two functions of fats in the diet.
....

6. Name two water soluble vitamins.
....

7. Which vitamin helps the absorption of iron?
....

8. Which vitamin helps with the absorption of calcium?
....

9. Why would an athlete require the B group of vitamins in the diet?
....

10. Why is folic acid important in the diet of pregnant women?
....

11. State one function of iron in the body.
....

12. State two functions of calcium in the body.
....

13. What is the effect of having too much sodium in the diet?
....

14. List four food sources of sodium.
....

15. Give two reasons why we need water in our diet.
....

16. Explain the difference between HBV and LBV proteins.
....

17. How does omega 3 contribute to good health?
....

CREDIT

18. Name the antioxidant vitamins.
....

19. Give two explanations why a diet high in antioxidants contributes to good health.
....

20. Name one substance which hinders the absorption of calcium in the body.
....

21. Name one substance which hinders the absorption of iron in the body.
....

How did you do?

19–21 correct	Excellent
14–18 correct	Good work
8–13 correct	Getting there
1–7 correct	Start again

Answers

1. A balanced diet provides all the necessary nutrients in the correct proportions and quantities to meet our needs.

2. Any 2 answers: growth of body tissues/cells in children; repair of body tissues/cells in children and adults; maintenance of body tissues; excess protein can be used as a source of energy.

3. Energy for all activities or warmth – excess carbohydrates that are not used for energy can be converted into body fat and so can provide warmth.

4. Cereals, e.g. oats, rice; cereal foods, e.g. bread, pasta, breakfast cereals; vegetables, e.g. potatoes or lentils.

5. Any 2 answers: provides a very concentrated source of energy; provides warmth – excess fat is stored under the skin providing an insulating layer; provides a source of fat soluble vitamins A, D E and K; provides essential fatty acids especially omega 3.

6. Vitamin C and vitamin B complex.

7. Vitamin C.

8. Vitamin D.

9. Because it helps release energy from food/protein/carbohydrates/fats and athletes require a lot of energy.

10. Needed for the formation of red blood cells; helps protect against neural tube defects such as spina bifida in unborn babies.

11. Any 1 answer: required for formation of red blood cells; red blood cells (haemoglobin) carry oxygen round the body; prevents anaemia.

12. Any 2 answers: aids growth and development of bones and teeth preventing rickets in children; helps in the normal clotting of blood; required for the normal functioning of muscles and nerves; combines with phosphorus to give calcium phosphate which gives bones and teeth their hardness.

13. High blood pressure.

14. Bacon, cheese, salt, convenience foods, savoury snacks, e.g. crisps.

15. Any 2 answers: it is required for all our body fluids (e.g. blood, urine); it helps in the removal of waste products from all our body tissues and organs; nearly all our body processes need water for them to take place, e.g. digestion, absorption of nutrients; it helps to regulate body temperature.

16. HBV proteins contain all the 8 essential amino acids required for growth, repair and maintenance; LBV proteins tend to lack one or more of the essential amino acids.

17. Omega 3 is an important essential fatty acid as it reduces the risk of blood clots forming and so lessens the risk of heart disease and strokes.

18. Vitamins A, C and E.

19. These vitamins can help reduce the risk of heart disease; these vitamins can help reduce the risk of cancers.

20. Dietary fibre/NSP, phytic acid, fats or oxalic acid, low intake of vitamin D.

21. Dietary fibre/NSP, phytic acid, low intake of vitamin C.

Current dietary advice 1

Dietary targets

People in Scotland have been given a set of dietary targets to help to improve their eating habits. These targets should be considered along with other factors that determine appropriate food intake (see page 33).

There are **eight dietary targets** related to food for the general population.

Top Tip
If you are already achieving some of these targets, you don't need to increase your intake to meet them.

Food	Target
Fruit and vegetables	Intake to **double to 400g per day**. This is approximately five portions per day and can be eaten as fresh, frozen, canned or dried fruit and vegetables. One portion could be a glass of fresh fruit juice, a bowl of vegetable soup, 100g vegetables, a large salad.
Bread	Intake to **increase by 45%** from present average daily intake, mainly using wholemeal and brown bread. Depending on the type and size of bread this could be equal to 4–6 slices each day.
Breakfast cereals	Intake to **double to 34g per day**. This is roughly equal to one bowl per day.
Total complex	Intake to increase by a quarter **(25%)** by eating more fruit and vegetables; also wholemeal bread, wholegrain breakfast cereals, brown rice and wholemeal pasta. Potato consumption to increase by **25%**.
Fish	Intake of white fish to be maintained. Intake of oily fish to **double from 44g to 88g per week.**
Fats	Average intake of total fat to be reduced to **no more than 35% of food energy**. Average intake of saturated fat to be reduced to **no more than 11% of food energy**.
Salt	Average daily intake to reduce to **100mmol per day (about 6g salt)**.
Sugar	Adult intake of non-milk extrinsic (NME) sugars not to rise. Children's intake of NME sugars to reduce by half **to less than 10% of food energy**.

There is also an **additional dietary target** for **newborn babies**: breastfeeding is to be encouraged in the first 6 weeks of a baby's life. The proportion of mothers who breastfeed their babies in the first 6 weeks of life should increase to **more than 50%**.

Top Tip
The words on **yellow backgrounds** are helpful for Credit level.

Choice of cooking methods

Top Tip
°Use the word **ASH** to help you remember **A**lkalinity, **S**olubility and **H**eat.

Choosing the correct foods to eat is important when trying to follow current dietary advice but so is choosing the correct method of cooking.

Methods of cooking to reduce fat intake

- No fat is added during: grilling, baking, boiling, steaming, microwave cooking, pressure cooking, poaching.
- Fat is removed during: grilling.

Some methods of cooking, such as shallow frying and deep fat frying, **add fat** to the food. These methods should not be used too often. Stir frying also adds fat during cooking, but if olive oil and plenty of vegetables are used, it can contribute to good health.

Methods of cooking to retain the vitamins in food

Some methods of cooking will result in loss of vitamins, especially the water soluble B group of vitamins and vitamin C.

Three factors affect the vitamin content of food:

Factor	Effect
Alkalinity	Vitamin C will be lost if an **alkaline** like bicarbonate of soda is added to the water when cooking. Vitamin B1 will be reduced if a **raising agent** is added to some baked foods.
Solubility	Because the B group of vitamins and vitamin C are **water** soluble, they: • **leach out** into the water and are lost unless the water is used for soup or sauces • are lost if cooked in **too much water** or for **too long**. Vitamins A and D dissolve in **fat**, so they are lost during **grilling** when the fat drips off food.
Heat	Both vitamin B complex and vitamin C are lost due to heat during cooking: • vitamin B complex is lost at **high temperatures**, e.g. boiling point • vitamin C is lost at **lower temperatures** (lower than boiling point).

Steaming, **pressure** and **microwave cooking** may help prevent loss of vitamins as food is either cooked very quickly or little or no water is used.

Top Tip
The methods of cooking using water – boiling, stewing, poaching – are more likely to result in loss of the water soluble vitamins, B complex and C.

Quick Test

1. How can you increase your total complex carbohydrate intake?
2. What types of bread should you eat?
3. How much energy should children receive from sugar?
4. Which method of cooking removes fat during cooking?
5. What does ASH stand for?

Answers 1. By eating more fruit and vegetables, bread, breakfast cereals, rice, pasta and potatoes. **2.** Wholemeal or brown. **3.** Less than 10% of energy. **4.** Grilling. **5.** Alkalinity, solubility, heat.

Current dietary advice 2

Ways to meet current dietary targets

Now that you know what the dietary targets are, how can you meet them? Here are some examples.

Increasing intakes

Increasing vegetable intake
- Have salads
- Have vegetables with each meal
- Add vegetables to dishes, e.g. chilli
- Use in healthy soups, e.g. carrot and coriander
- Eat raw as snacks

Increasing fruit intake
- Eat fruit as a snack
- Use fresh fruit in drinks, e.g. fruit juice drinks, smoothies
- Add fruit to baked products, e.g. muffins
- Use fruit as a base for puddings, e.g. fruit salad

Increasing bread intake
- Eat wholemeal bread/rolls instead of white in sandwiches
- Use wholemeal breadcrumbs when providing bulk, e.g. beefburgers
- Eat a wider selection of breads such as continental breads

Increasing fish intake
- Use a variety of fish for starters, e.g. prawn cocktail, tuna pate and toast
- Use fish as a substitute for meat in some dishes, e.g. salads, stir fries
- Eat oily fish in a wide variety of ways, e.g. sandwiches, pizzas, ready meals

Increasing breakfast cereal intake
- Eat a bowl of wholegrain breakfast cereal every morning or in the evening as a snack
- Use wholegrain cereals in baking, e.g. muesli bars or dessert toppings
- Use crushed breakfast cereals as a coating for food to be fried or baked, e.g. crispy baked chicken

Increasing total complex carbohydrate intake
- Use rice or pasta in meals
- Add pulses, rice, pasta to homemade soups
- Use wholemeal flour when baking instead of white flour
- Eat wholegrain breakfast cereals instead of sugary/refined cereals

Reducing intakes

Reducing salt intake
- Do not add salt to any meals at the table
- Season foods (add flavour) by using herbs and spices instead of salt
- Use low salt versions of products which are available in supermarkets – look at the labels
- Limit the use of stock cubes and soy sauce as these contain a lot of salt.

Top Tip
Of the eight dietary targets related to food, five increase consumption and three reduce consumption – fats, sugar and salt. Remember this!

Reducing fat intake

- Choose low fat products, e.g. mayonnaise, yoghurts
- Choose lean cuts or types of meat and trim any visible fat from meat
- Do not add fat to food, e.g. glazing carrots with butter
- Skim off any fat from mince, stews, soups, gravies, etc.

Reducing sugar intake

- Drink sugar free, low calorie drinks or water
- Eat fruit as a snack rather than sweets or cakes
- Choose fruit tinned in natural juice instead of in syrup
- Reduce the amount of sugar used in recipes for baking and use dried fruit or artificial sweeteners.

Top Tip
In your exam you may be given a recipe or menu which you have to adapt to make it healthier and link with dietary targets.

How to adapt foods to meet dietary advice

Here are some examples of how you can adapt some foods in line with dietary targets.

Foods	Change to	Reason
Fried fish	Poached salmon	• Increase intake of oily fish. • Method of cooking (poaching) will help to reduce fat intake.
Deep fried chips	Baked potato, potato wedges, oven chips	• Cooking method reduces fat intake. • Increases total complex carbohydrate intake.
Cola drink	Water Semi-skimmed milk Fresh fruit juice	• Reduces sugar intake. • Semi-skimmed milk has less fat than full fat milk. • Fruit juice increases fruit intake.
Crisps	Fruit Low fat crisps Salt free crisps	• Increases fruit intake/reduces fat intake • Reduces fat intake • Reduces salt intake

Quick Test

Complete the following chart.

Foods	Change to	Reason
Corned beef sandwich using white bread		
Sugar-coated breakfast cereals		

Diet and health

Dietary diseases

Meeting the dietary targets will help to prevent the following dietary diseases.

Anaemia

Causes	Effect on health	Notes
Lack of iron (iron deficient anaemia).	• Tiredness. • Breathlessness. • Dizziness, fast pulse.	• Common form of anaemia in teenagers, especially girls, due to menstruation.
Lack of vitamin B12 (vitamin B12 deficient anaemia).	• Abnormal nervous reactions. • Depression, confusion. • Colour blindness.	• Found only in animal sources so can be lacking in vegan diets.
Lack of folic acid (folic acid deficient anaemia).	• Foetal abnormalities (spina bifida). • Neurological abnormalities in infants.	• Important for pregnant women, before becoming pregnant and also for the first 12 weeks of pregnancy.

Bowel disorders: constipation, haemorrhoids, diverticular disease

Causes	Effect on health	Notes
Diet related causes: being overweight, not eating enough NSP, insufficient liquid intake, eating too many processed foods. **Lifestyle related causes:** not exercising enough.	• Constipation. • Haemorrhoids (piles) (which are enlarged blood vessels around the back passage with pain and bleeding). • Diverticular disease (weakness of bowel lining in the lower part of the large intestine).	People most at risk are: • overweight • women during and after pregnancy • people with heavy lifting jobs • people who are prone to constipation • people who eat a lot of refined/processed foods.

Cancer

Causes	Effect on health	Notes
Diet related causes: diets high in fat (saturated fat intake has been related to breast cancer), high in calories; diets low in NSP. **Lifestyle related causes:** smoking, high alcohol intake. **Other causes:** hereditary factors, age, gender.	Cancer cells are formed when the process of cell division goes wrong – new cells are formed unnecessarily and lead to the growth of a tumour or cancer. 	Steps can be taken which may prevent certain types of cancer; these include: eat a diet rich in fruit, vegetables and wholegrain cereals which contain vitamins A, C and E, as well as NSP.

Coronary heart disease (CHD)

Causes	Effect on health	Notes
Diet related causes: being overweight, having high blood pressure; diets high in saturated fat and salt. **Lifestyle related causes:** stress, smoking, insufficient exercise, high alcohol intake. **Other causes:** hereditary factors, increasing age, gender	• Eating too many saturated fats can increase levels of **cholesterol** (fatty deposits) in the blood. • CHD occurs when cholesterol sticks to the heart's own artery walls and reduces the amount of blood reaching the heart. • Symptoms include severe chest pain (angina), heart attack and possibly death.	Steps which can be taken to prevent CHD: • reduce overall fat intake • replace saturated fats with polyunsaturated fats • a diet rich in vitamins A, C and E will help stop cholesterol sticking to the artery walls • reduce alcohol intake.

Hypertension and strokes

Causes	Effect on health	Notes
Diet related causes: diet high in salt; being overweight. **Lifestyle related causes:** lack of exercise, high alcohol intake. **Other causes:** race, hereditary factors, increasing age, gender, medication.	• Thickening and hardening of artery walls causes the heart to work harder. This causes high blood pressure as well as making the heart more prone to injury. • A stroke may be the result of a blood clot. If a blood clot forms in an artery it can reduce or block blood supply to parts of the body, and the brain. • High blood pressure can lead to CHD.	• Hypertension is another name for high blood pressure. • The risk of high blood pressure and strokes increases with age. Normal artery with good blood flow Artery with fatty deposits leading to increase blood presure and possible risk blood clot

Tooth decay

Causes	Effect on health	Notes
Diet related causes: eating and drinking sweet foods/drinks; diet low in calcium, phosphorus and vitamin D. **Lifestyle related causes:** lack of good dental hygiene.	• The food you eat feeds the bacteria on your teeth and forms **plaque**, which is the main cause of tooth decay and gum disease. • If your diet is poor it will be harder for the tissues of your mouth to resist infection, which can lead to gum disease.	• Tooth decay is sometimes called dental caries. • Plaque can be removed by regularly brushing your teeth or flossing after every meal as well as morning and night. • Use fluoride toothpaste to strengthen tooth enamel. • Visit the dentist every 6 months. • Choose nuts, raw vegetables, sugarless gum for snacks.

Current dietary advice in relation to good health

Weight control and obesity

Causes	Effect on health	Notes
Diet related causes: diets high in fats and sugars, and low in NSP; eating more calories/energy than is used up by activities.	Being overweight can lead to a variety of medical problems such as:	• It is important to balance the amount of energy you eat with the amount you use – **energy balance**. If you use less than you take in, it can lead to weight gain and perhaps obesity.
Lifestyle related causes: lack of exercise to burn off energy from foods.	• high blood pressure • strokes • heart disease • diabetes • gallstones • some types of cancer.	• If you need to lose weight, do so sensibly by eating foods that are less energy rich and take more exercise.

Top Tip

All this information can be used to answer questions in many different ways. For example, you know that one **cause** of obesity is a diet low in NSP because you feel hungry more quickly, which can lead to more frequent snacking on sugary or fatty foods. You can turn this knowledge around to describe one way of preventing obesity – have a diet high in NSP which, because NSP is filling, will prevent you snacking too often on sugary or fatty foods.

Quick Test

1. State two causes of bowel disorders.
2. What is another name for high blood pressure?
3. How can a diet high in NSP prevent obesity?
4. Name one cause of tooth decay.

Food labelling

Food labelling can help you choose foods which contribute to a healthy diet.

It is important to remember that there are laws and guidelines about labelling to tell consumers what they are buying. The chart below explains some of the nutritional information which can be found on product labels.

Nutritional information allows you to compare the nutritional value of similar products. It is **voluntary**, unless a manufacturer is making a specific nutritional claim, e.g. low in fat.

Top Tip
Keep up to date with food labelling because food manufacturers frequently change how their food labels look.

Top Tip
Check out the Food Standards Agency website for updates on nutritional labelling. Go to the Leckie & Leckie website www.leckieand leckie.co.uk

Nutritional information	Notes
Energy Protein Carbohydrate Fat	Most manufacturers will display this nutritional information on their products.
Carbohydrates • of which sugars Fat • of which saturates • of which polyunsaturates Fibre Salt/sodium	Some labels give extra information which is helpful to diabetics, people with high cholesterol levels or high blood pressure.
Typical value per 100g/100ml	This information **must** be shown to link with the nutritional information displayed.
Typical value per serving	This is very useful information as some average servings will be more or less than 100g/100ml.
Low sugar or Low fat	Manufacturers **must** provide nutritional information to support this claim. **Read labels carefully**: what you think is healthy might not be, e.g. a food advertised as low in fat might contain a lot of sugar and so be high in calories.
Healthy choices	More food manufacturers identify products which are healthy choices, e.g. tick system, traffic lights labelling system (red/amber/green). Some manufacturers show how much a portion of their product contributes to the recommended daily intake of a nutrient.

Quick Test

1. State two benefits of food labelling to the consumer.
2. Is nutritional labelling always voluntary?
3. Which groups of people would find additional nutritional information particularly useful?

Answers 1. Food labelling can help the consumer choose foods which contribute to a healthy diet; it also allows consumers to compare the nutritional value of similar products. **2.** Yes, unless a nutritional claim is being made. **3.** Diabetics, people with high cholesterol levels or high blood pressure.

Test your progress

Use the questions to test your progress.

1. Why have people in Scotland been given a set of dietary targets as guidance? . . . .
. . . .

2. Which five targets should we increase our consumption of? . . . .
. . . .

3. Which dietary targets should we decrease our consumption of? . . . .
. . . .

4. What is the least amount of time that mothers are advised to breastfeed? . . . .
. . . .

5. Which type of fat would be the best to use when stir frying? . . . .
. . . .

6. Which vitamins can be easily lost during cooking? . . . .
. . . .

7. List three methods of cooking which keep vitamins in foods best. . . . .
. . . .

8. **a)** List the three factors which will affect the vitamin content of food during cooking.
. . . .

   b) Explain each of these factors in detail. . . . .
. . . .

9. Give two practical ways of increasing breakfast cereal intake. . . . .
. . . .

10. Describe two ways to reduce the fat intake in the diet. . . . .
. . . .

11. What is the most common cause of anaemia and what are the symptoms? . . . .
. . . .

12. Which two foods would help a pregnant woman who suffers from constipation? . . . .
. . . .

13. Which vitamins may help prevent cancer? . . . .
. . . .

14. List three factors which could contribute to heart disease. . . . .
. . . .

15. What dietary factor may cause cholesterol levels in the blood to rise? . . . .
. . . .

16. State two pieces of advice you would give to help prevent heart disease. . . . .
. . . .

17. List two causes of hypertension. . . . .
. . . .

18. How is plaque formed in the mouth? . . . .
. . . .

19. List three possible effects on health of being obese. . . . .
. . . .

20. What is meant by 'energy balance' in preventing obesity? . . . .
. . . .

21. If a food product claims to be 'low in fat', what information must manufacturers give
to consumers? . . . .
. . . .

How did you do?

19–21 correct	Excellent
14–18 correct	Good work
8–13 correct	Getting there
1–7 correct	Start again

Answers

1. To help to improve their eating habits.

2. Fruit and vegetables, bread, breakfast cereals total complex carbohydrates and fish.

3. Fats, salt and sugar.

4. 6 weeks.

5. Olive oil.

6. Vitamins C and B complex.

7. Steaming, pressure cooking and microwave cooking.

8. **a)** Alkalinity, solubility and heat;
   b) Alkalinity: vitamin C is lost if an alkaline like bicarbonate of soda is added to the water when cooking or vitamin B1 will be reduced if a raising agent is added to some baked foods; Solubility: vitamin B complex and C dissolve in water and leach out into the water and are lost or are lost if cooked in too much water or for too long; vitamins A and D dissolve in fat and can be lost when the fat drips during grilling of food; Heat: both vitamin B complex and vitamin C are lost due to heat during cooking (vitamin B complex at high temperatures, e.g. boiling. point, and vitamin C at lower temperatures).

9. Any 2 answers: eating a bowl of wholegrain breakfast cereal every morning or in the evening or as a snack; using wholegrain cereals in baking, e.g. muesli bars or topping for desserts; using crushed breakfast cereals as a coating for food to be fried or baked, e.g. crispy baked chicken.

10. Any 2 answers: choosing low fat products, e.g. mayonnaise, yoghurts; choosing lean cuts or types of meat or trim any visible fat from meat; not adding additional fat to food, e.g. glazing carrots with butter; skimming off any fat from mince, stews, soups, gravies, etc.

11. Lack of iron; symptoms include tiredness, breathlessness, dizziness, fast pulse.

12. Wholegrain cereals such as oats, wheat, rice, wholemeal bread; fruit (with skins on) and vegetables particularly leafy vegetables.

13. The antioxidant vitamins/vitamins A, C and E.

14. Any 3 answers: being overweight; having high blood pressure; stress; smoking; insufficient exercise; high alcohol intake; hereditary factors/age and gender.

15. Any 1 answer: eating too much saturated fats; not having sufficient vitamins A, C or E; insufficient polyunsaturated fats.

16. Any 2 answers: reduce fat intake; have sufficient vitamins A, C, E to help stop cholesterol sticking to the artery walls; Increase intake of polyunsaturated fats to help reduce the risk of blood clots and so reduce the risk of heart attacks; lower intake of salt which would help prevent HBP which could lead to heart disease.

17. Any 2 answers: diet high in salt; being overweight; high intake of alcohol; lack of exercise; race; age/gender; medication; family history.

18. The food you eat feeds the bacteria on your teeth and forms plaque.

19. Any 3 answers: high blood pressure, strokes, heart disease, diabetes, gall stones or certain cancers.

20. It is balancing the amount of energy you eat with the amount of energy you use.

21. Nutritional information.

Dietary requirements 1

Dietary Reference Values

Dietary Reference Values (DRVs) are the estimated amount of each nutrient and energy intake that different groups of people need to be healthy.

CREDIT

DRVs include the following two terms:

- **Reference Nutrient Intake** (RNI): the amount of a nutrient that is sufficient for most people
- **Estimated Average Requirements** (EAR): the average need for a nutrient. Some people will need more, some will need less

Top Tip
In the Credit paper – Handling Information - the figures for RNIs and EARs for nutrients and energy are given to you to evaluate for a specific group of people. To successfully answer this question, you must know the sources and functions of each nutrient.

Infants

Infants grow very quickly during the first few weeks of life so a nutritious diet is very important. One of the dietary targets encourages **breastfeeding** for a variety of reasons:

- breast milk provides all the nutrients required by a baby
- these nutrients are in a form that are easy to digest so there is less risk of stomach upsets
- breast milk contains antibodies which can help the infant fight infections
- the baby is less likely to become overweight, or develop allergies or asthma
- breastfeeding helps develop a bond between mother and baby
- breastfeeding is less expensive than bottle feeding.

Breastfeeding is good for a mother as well because it uses extra energy, helping her to lose weight gained during pregnancy. It is also thought that breastfeeding mothers are less likely to develop breast cancer.

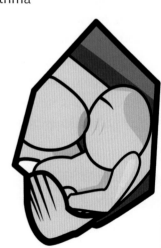

If an infant is bottle fed, care must be taken to give the correct amount of infant formula:

- to prevent over feeding
- to ensure good hygiene during preparation, to lessen the risk of stomach upsets.

Babies can be **weaned** onto solid food from breast or bottle milk but no earlier than **4 months** of age. Foods used in weaning should not contain any added salt or sugar.

Children

Good eating habits are formed in childhood, so a healthy varied diet should be encouraged, with a careful watch on the amount of sugar, fat and salt consumed. The **most important nutrients** needed at this stage are:

Nutrient	Reason why each nutrient is needed
Protein	Children grow rapidly, so protein is required for growth, repair and maintenance of cells and tissues. Protein is needed to repair cuts and wounds.
Carbohydrates	Children are usually very energetic. Carbohydrates, especially total complex carbohydrates, release energy slowly.
Calcium, phosphorus, and vitamin D	Childhood is an important age for bone and teeth development.
Iron	Iron is important for healthy blood – so that the oxygen carried in the blood reaches all the body cells and prevents a feeling of tiredness. If a child is very active their body cells need more oxygen (they may need to increase their intake of iron).
Vitamin C	Vitamin C helps iron absorption and therefore oxygen transport around the body. Vitamin C also helps form connective tissues, helping wounds to heal.

Top Tip

Young children should be served small, attractive meals with a variety of flavours and textures to encourage them to eat a varied diet.

Adolescents

Many adolescents do not eat a balanced diet, having diets high in energy dense foods and low in nutritive value, often the result of eating too many snack and fast foods. The **most important nutrients** required at this stage are:

Nutrient	Reason why each nutrient is needed
Protein	Protein is required to cope with the 'growth spurt' of teenagers, to repair damaged tissues and for maintenance of cells and tissues.
Carbohydrates	As the body frame grows there is an increased demand for energy. Teenagers vary in the amount of energy used depending on the sports they play and activities they do.
Calcium, phosphorus, and vitamin D	Adolescence is an important time for bone development and maintenance.
Iron	Blood volume increases as adolescents grow so more iron is required to prevent anaemia in both boys and girls. Teenage girls need to increase iron intake, especially when menstruation starts.
Vitamin C	Vitamin C is important to ensure the absorption of iron and prevent anaemia.
Vitamin B complex	If adolescents are active then this vitamin will release the energy from foods.

Quick Test

1. Explain the term EAR.
2. State an advantage to mothers of breastfeeding their babies.
3. Why do some adolescents not eat a varied diet?
4. List two nutrients of particular importance to children.

Answers 1. Estimated Average Requirement – the average need for a nutrient: some people will need more, some will need less. **2.** May help them lose them weight gained during pregnancy; help bond with baby. **3.** Because they eat too many snack foods. **4.** Protein, carbohydrates, calcium, phosphorus, vitamin D, iron, vitamin C.

Dietary requirements 2

Adults

During adulthood, body growth has stopped and people tend to become less active, so their energy needs generally decrease. The **most important nutrients** at this stage are:

Nutrient	Reason why each nutrient is needed
Protein	To repair and maintain cells and tissues.
Carbohydrates	Adults have stopped growing and are sometimes less active so require less energy. The activity level of individual adults should be considered, with intake balancing requirements.
Calcium, phosphorus, vitamin D	Adulthood is an important time for bone maintenance; these nutrients will help prevent osteoporosis in later life.
Iron, vitamin C	Iron and vitamin C are needed to prevent anaemia. A woman's iron requirements reduce when she stops menstruating.

Intake of the following nutrients should be limited:

Sodium/salt	Salt intake should be reduced to help prevent high blood pressure.
Fats	Less fats should be eaten, especially saturated fats. This will reduce the risk of obesity and heart disease.

Top Tip
Adults and the elderly need some of the same nutrients, but the reasons why they need them may be slightly different.

Elderly

It is important that the elderly eat a balanced diet to help them stay fit and active.

The **most important nutrients** at this stage are:

Nutrient	Reason why each nutrient is needed
Protein	To repair and maintain cells and tissues. Elderly people suffer more from ill health, and protein may be used to help recovery.
Carbohydrates	Overall energy needs reduce as people age, but the percentage supplied by TCC should increase. Carbohydrates containing dietary fibre/NSP are important to prevent constipation. Less sugars should be eaten to prevent obesity.
Calcium, phosphorus, vitamin D	These are important to maintain healthy bones, to prevent bone diseases which are common in the elderly: ● osteoporosis – a brittle bone disease resulting from poor calcium absorption ● osteomalacia – a disease caused by lack of vitamin D, where the strength of bones is not maintained.
Iron, vitamin C	Elderly people may not eat a balanced diet, missing out on these nutrients, so may be more likely to develop anaemia.

CREDIT

Intake of the following nutrients should be limited:

Sodium/salt	Salt intake should be reduced to help prevent high blood pressure.
Fats	Less fats should be eaten, especially saturated fats. This reduces the risk of weight gain and heart disease.

People with special needs or beliefs

Some people have different dietary requirements, not because of their age, but because their bodies have special needs, or because they have particular beliefs.

Pregnant women

The diet of a pregnant woman must meet her nutritional needs **and** those of the developing baby. The **most important dietary** needs during pregnancy are:

Nutrient	Reason why each nutrient is needed
Protein	A little more protein will be needed to help the unborn baby's cells and tissues to grow.
Carbohydrates	Towards the end of the pregnancy, the unborn baby will require extra energy for growth and as it becomes more active so a little extra carbohydrate can be eaten.
Iron	No additional iron should be needed as menstruation stops. However the diet must contain good sources of iron as the baby will require iron to have as a store during the first few weeks of life.
Vitamin C	Vitamin C helps iron absorption, which the baby needs for tissue formation.
Folic acid	Foods rich in folic acid should be consumed before and during pregnancy – especially the first three months of pregnancy. This could be taken in the form of fortified foods or supplements. This will prevent spina bifida in the baby and anaemia in the mother.
Calcium, phosphorus, vitamin D	Sufficient must be consumed to ensure that baby's bones develop correctly and no calcium is taken from the mother's bones.

Other factors pregnant women should remember:

- Pregnant women are prone to constipation, so a good supply of dietary fibre/NSP and adequate water intake is required to prevent this.
- Due to their high vitamin A content, liver and liver pate should be avoided during pregnancy as they can harm the baby.
- Some foods should be avoided as they are harmful to the developing baby: these include certain chilled foods, such as soft cheeses and pate (may contain listeria bacteria), and raw eggs and raw egg products (may contain salmonella bacteria).

Top Tip
Cook chill foods such as ready meals must be thoroughly cooked as they may contain listeria bacteria which could harm the unborn baby.

Quick Test

1. Why should the elderly limit sodium intake?
2. Which nutrients affect bone strength in adults?
3. Why is diet during pregnancy important?
4. Why should pregnant women eat a little more protein?

Answers 1. To reduce the risk of high blood pressure. **2.** Calcium, phosphorus and vitamin D. **3.** Because it can affect the health of both mother and unborn baby. **4.** To help the unborn baby's cells and tissues to grow.

Dietary requirements 3

Vegetarians

Some people become vegetarian for religious, ethical or moral reasons. Some believe that a vegetarian diet is healthier, while others simply dislike the taste of meat.

There are two main types of vegetarians:

- **Lactovegetarians** eat milk, cheese and dairy products but do not eat meat, fish or eggs (ovo-lactovegetarians do eat eggs as well as dairy products)

- **Vegans** do not eat any animals or animal products such as eggs, milk, cheese.

Nutrient	Lactovegetarian	Vegan
Protein	 Obtained from cheese and milk. Foods which are suitable for vegans can also be eaten by this group.	As protein will be obtained only from plant sources, it will be LBV protein, so a variety of foods must be combined to make up for the shortage of essential amino acids. Textured vegetable protein, a protein made from a plant source is high in protein, low in fat and is a source of dietary fibre/NSP.
Calcium	Milk and cheese are good sources of calcium so bone development and maintenance may continue unimpaired.	Calcium may be deficient as phytic acid, present in wholegrain cereals, may hinder the absorption of calcium. Soya milk and products will provide calcium.
Vitamin B12	Found in a variety of animal products and foods, e.g. milk.	Fortified foods or supplements should be eaten to ensure adequate intake.
Fats	Cheese and milk are eaten, perhaps in higher quantities than in non-vegetarian diets, so it is possible that the saturated fat content of the diet could be too high, unless low fat options are chosen.	Vegans will eat less saturated fat as no animal food sources are eaten. They are likely to eat more polyunsaturated fats in the form of vegetable oils and margarine, reducing the risk of heart disease.
Carbohydrate	Eaten by both types of vegetarians but vegans may eat more total complex carbohydrate. If these are good sources of dietary fibre/NSP (fruit, vegetables, pulses), then this is beneficial to health.	

Quick Test

1. Name two types of vegetarians.
2. What may hinder the absorption of calcium?
3. What is an LBV food? (Check back to page 8.)

Answers 1. Lactovegetarians and vegans. **2.** Phytic acid. **3.** A food that is missing one or more of the essential amino acids.

Factors affecting food choice

In addition to dietary requirements, there are a number of factors that will affect the suitability of food choices made by individuals.

Body size

Generally, the larger the body size the more energy is needed. Basal Metabolic Rate (BMR) is the amount of energy needed when the body is resting, e.g. breathing, digestion.

Age

As people become older, they are generally less active and their BMR is lower, so they use less energy. Energy intake should be reduced accordingly.

Gender

Men generally have a larger body size and are heavier than women, so need more energy. Men may need more protein to develop and maintain muscles.

Available income

The amount of income available for food will affect the quality and type of food purchased. A low income may cause purchase of less fruit and vegetables and more fatty and sugary foods. High income doesn't always lead to good diet.

Health

As well as pregnant women and vegetarians, other groups in the population have to consider additional dietary factors to maintain good health:

- A **woman who is breastfeeding** needs:
    - an increase in energy and nutrients for breastfeeding
    - to ensure that sufficient protein, calcium, iron, vitamins A, C, D and B group are eaten and sufficient water is drunk.
- An **invalid** has reduced energy needs but still requires protein, calcium, iron and vitamins A, D and C to repair and maintain the body tissues.
- A person on a **weight reducing diet** needs to eat a balanced diet, even if overall calorie intake is restricted.

Lifestyle/occupation

People who are **active**, whether by occupation or leisure activities, should ensure their diets meet their nutritional needs, with adequate intake of protein, vitamin B, iron and vitamin C. Less active people should reduce energy intake.

Quick Test

1. How does age affect energy intake?
2. Why do men usually need more energy than women?
3. State one piece of advice for sensible weight loss.

Answers 1. As people age, they need less energy because they are generally less active and their metabolism rate decreases. **2.** Men generally have a larger body size and are heavier than women, so more energy is required for activity. **3.** A balanced diet must be eaten.

Test your progress

Use the questions to test your progress.

1. Give two reasons why breastfeeding should be encouraged.

   . . . .

2. What is the minimum age for weaning babies?

   . . . .

3. Why is vitamin C important to children?

   . . . .

4. Why do children need calcium, phosphorus and vitamin D?

   . . . .

5. Give two reasons why adolescents require protein.

   . . . .

6. Name two nutrients the elderly should reduce in their diet.

   . . . .

7. Why should pregnant women avoid eating products containing raw eggs?

   . . . .

8. Explain the importance of folic acid during pregnancy.

   . . . .

9. Why do pregnant women need iron?

   . . . .

10. Give two reasons why people may become vegetarians.

    . . . .

11. Which vitamin may be deficient in the diet of a vegan?

    . . . .

12. How does the fat intake of a lactovegetarian differ from that of a vegan?

    . . . .

13. Name two sources of protein suitable for a vegan.

    . . . .

14. How does body size affect suitable food choice?

    . . . .

15. Explain how food choice may be affected by income.

    . . . .

16. State two nutritional requirements of a woman who is breastfeeding.

    . . . .

17. State two nutritional requirements of an invalid.

    . . . .

18. State and explain two nutritional requirements of active people.

    . . . .

19. Explain the term RNI.

    . . . .

20. Explain the term osteoporosis.

    . . . .

21. Explain the term osteomalacia.

    . . . .

CREDIT

Answers

1. Any 2 answers: breast milk provides all the nutrients required by a baby; these nutrients are in a form that are easy to digest so there is less risk of stomach upsets; breast milk contains antibodies which can help the infant fight infections; the baby is less likely to be overweight, develop allergies or asthma; a bond develops between mother and child; breast feeding is good for the mother as it may help her to lose any stores of fat gained during pregnancy; women who breastfeed appear to have lower rates of breast cancer.

2. 4 months.

3. It helps iron absorption so that children do not feel tired especially if active; it helps form connective tissue which helps wounds to heal.

4. Childhood is an important age for bone and teeth development.

5. Any 2 answers: protein is required to cope with the 'growth spurt'; repair damaged tissues; maintenance of cells and tissues.

6. Fat and sodium.

7. Raw eggs and raw egg products may contain salmonella bacteria which can harm the unborn baby.

8. Foods rich in folic acid should be consumed before and during pregnancy, especially in the first three months of pregnancy, in order to prevent spina bifida in the baby and anaemia in the mother.

9. The baby will require iron to have as a store during the first few weeks of life.

10. Any 2 answers: religious beliefs may affect type of foods that can be eaten; moral issues; dietary reasons – a belief that a vegetarian diet is more healthy; the taste of meat may be disliked.

11. Vitamin B12.

12. A lactovegetarian eats cheese and milk so it is possible that the saturated fat content of the diet could increase unless low fat options are chosen; a vegan will eat less saturated fat because they do not eat animal food sources, and they will eat more polyunsaturated fats in the form of vegetable oils and margarine.

13. Any 2 answers: soya, tofu, peas, beans and lentils.

14. Generally, larger bodies need more energy; tall, thin people have higher basal metabolic rate (BMR) and so burn energy more quickly than smaller, plump people.

15. The amount of income will affect the quality and type of food purchased; a low income may mean less fruit and vegetables but more fatty and sugary foods are purchased, but a high income does not necessarily mean that a more healthy diet may be eaten, as more high fat, protein rich foods may be purchased.

16. Any 2 answers: slight increase in energy, protein, calcium, iron, vitamins A, C, D and B group.

17. Any 2 answers: fats, sugar and starchy carbohydrate foods should be limited; protein, calcium, iron and vitamins A, D and C are required.

18. Any 2 answers: sufficient energy to allow for muscular activity; protein to allow for growth, maintenance and repair of tissues; vitamin B complex to release energy from foods; iron and vitamin C to ensure sufficient oxygen is transported round the body.

19. RNI is the amount of a nutrient that is sufficient for most people.

20. Osteoporosis is a brittle bone disease resulting from poor calcium absorption.

21. Osteomalacia is a disease where the strength of bones is not maintained due to lack of vitamin D.

Hygiene

General personal hygiene

Good **personal hygiene** helps you feel good, improves your self esteem, helps you make a good impression on others, and can improve your health, helping you fight illness and infection.

Clothes care

Clothes care contributes to good personal hygiene (washing away bacteria, perspiration, smoke and other odours absorbed by the fabric). An **international labelling system** ensures that clothing is laundered correctly. All garments have a **care label** with symbols/instructions.

Wash

- The temperature of the wash is shown below the water line.
- The amount of agitation is indicated by a bar below the tub, for example:

medium agitation   *minimal* agitation   hand wash only

Bleach

- Bleach is only used on white fabric.
- Chlorine bleach can be used if indicated by

Top Tip
Any care symbol with a X through it means DO NOT.

Dry

There are a variety of ways to dry clothes to ensure the fibres in clothing are not damaged, for example:

tumble dry   dry flat   line dry   drip dry

Iron

Some items of clothing need to be ironed at the correct **temperature**, to prevent clothes from being scorched (burnt and blackened) or melted.

cool   warm   hot

Dry clean

If clothing has difficult stains, is made of a special fabric or cannot be cleaned with detergent and water, dry cleaning is advised.

dry clean in all solvents   information only for professional dry cleaners

Hygiene in relation to food preparation

Food hygiene describes the practices we use to make sure food is safe to eat. There are two different aspects involved:

- **personal hygiene** – keeping you clean
- **kitchen hygiene** – keeping your workspace clean.

Personal hygiene

Personal hygiene rule	Reason
Hands and nails must be clean.	• Unclean hands can spread bacteria. • Nail varnish can chip into food.
Hair must be tied back and covered.	• To prevent hair from falling into food.
Do not wear jewellery.	• Stones can fall out and contaminate food. • Bacteria can breed in jewellery.
Wear a clean apron/overall. Wash it daily. Wear protective clothing only in the kitchen.	• It covers normal clothing to prevent transfer of bacteria. • Daily washing ensures coverings are clean and don't spread bacteria. • Wear only in the kitchen to prevent contamination from outside the kitchen.
Any cuts, boils must be covered with a blue waterproof plaster.	• Cuts and boils are a breeding ground for bacteria. • If the plaster falls off it can be easily seen.
Do not handle food if you are ill.	• Illness, coughing, sneezing can carry food poisoning bacteria.

Top Tip

In your exam read the question carefully (and think about your answer) to make sure you don't mix up personal hygiene with kitchen hygiene.

Kitchen hygiene

Kitchen hygiene rule	Reason
Wash food preparation areas with hot soapy water before and after use.	• To ensure hygienic food preparation surfaces.
The kitchen environment should have hand washing facilities and good lighting; toilet facilities should not be near the kitchen.	• To prevent the spread of bacteria and allow a good hygiene routine to be set up.
Dispose of all waste into covered bins.	• To prevent the spread of bacteria or attracting any pests.
Cover food at all times.	• To prevent contamination by bacteria or insects.
Do not allow animals into areas where food is prepared.	• Animals carry bacteria. • To prevent animal hairs from getting into food.
Wipe spills up immediately.	• To prevent bacteria from multiplying and spreading. • It is safer to wipe up spills (fewer slippery surfaces).

Top Tip

You usually have to give a reason for each rule.

Quick Test

1. How would you launder this garment?

2. Explain two personal hygiene rules and two kitchen hygiene rules to ensure safe food preparation.

Answers 1. A minimal wash at 40°C; do not bleach; use a hot iron or tumble dry; can be dry-cleaned. 2. Check your answers against the list above.

Food spoilage

Food spoilage organisms

Food spoilage is the process that results in food becoming unfit to eat. It is caused by different organisms.

Enzymes are natural chemicals found in food which can cause food to deteriorate in three ways:

Food spoilage is caused by

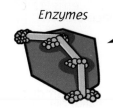
Enzymes

Micro-organisms

yeast

- **Ripening** – during storage, e.g. bananas go dark brown.
- **Browning** – certain foods react with the air and discolour, e.g. apples.
- **Oxidation** – vitamins A, C and B1 can be lost from food.

Yeasts are a type of fungus found in air, soil and on the surface of some fruits. Jams and meats can be affected by yeasts and they can influence the taste. Yeasts are used in the production of bread and wine. Heat will kill yeasts.

mould

Moulds are another sort of fungus which can cause food spoilage. They produce spores which are carried in the air and grow on the surface of food such as bread and cheese. Certain moulds produce harmful toxins (poisons) so food with mould should not be eaten. Moulds are killed by heat.

bacteria

Bacteria are single-celled organisms which we cannot see. They are found in air, in soil and on our bodies. Some bacteria are useful to us, e.g. in cheese making. Others can cause food spoilage and food poisoning. Some bacteria produce spores, which protect the bacteria from high temperatures. Spores do not multiply. When conditions are favourable the spores release the bacteria which can then start to multiply. Bacteria can produce toxins, which can make us very ill. Most bacteria can be killed by heat.

Top Tip
Bacterial growth can be slowed down or prevented if conditions are changed appropriately or removed altogether.

Conditions for bacterial growth

Bacteria need particular conditions for growth.

Temperature

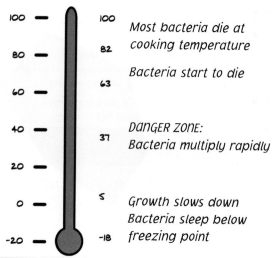

100	Most bacteria die at cooking temperature
82	Bacteria start to die
63	
37	DANGER ZONE: Bacteria multiply rapidly
5	Growth slows down
-18	Bacteria sleep below freezing point

In boiling water (100°C) most bacteria are killed in 1–2 minutes.

Above 63°C bacteria begin to die. It is important that any reheating of food is done thoroughly (reaching at least 82°C) so bacteria are killed.

Bacteria like the warmth and prefer to live at body temperature (37°C). This allows them to grow and multiply at a fast rate.

Low temperatures (below 4°C, e.g. normal refridgerator temperature) will either stop most bacteria growing or will slow their growth but will not kill them.

Food

Like all living cells, bacteria need food to grow. Foods can be classed as **high risk** or **low risk**.

High risk foods are sometimes called 'perishable foods' as they can 'go off' easily. They usually need to be stored in a refrigerator, and include:

- Foods high in protein, e.g. meat, fish
- Foods high in moisture, e.g. gravies, soups
- Foods that do not require any further heating, e.g.
  - all cooked meats, poultry and cooked meat products, e.g. pies, sausages
  - milk, cream, artificial cream, custard and dairy produce
  - egg products such as mayonnaise
  - shellfish and sea food
  - cooked rice.

Low risk foods do not supply the bacteria with the conditions they need to multiply, so there is less risk of food poisoning. They include:

- Foods high in salt, e.g. savoury snacks
- Foods high in sugar, e.g. jams
- Foods high in acid, e.g. pickled onions
- Foods high in fat, e.g. butter, lard
- Dry foods, e.g. biscuits, cereals.

This is why food preservation methods such as jam making, salting, pickling are so successful in preventing growth of bacteria.

Moisture

- Bacteria love moist foods, and require moisture for growth.
- Most foods contain some moisture, e.g. meat and chicken, so will support bacterial growth.
- The following foods are too dry for bacteria: flour, powdered milk, dried vegetables, sauce mixes, soup powders.
- Remember, if water is added to these foods and they are left for a period of time in warm conditions, bacteria will begin to multiply.

> **Top Tip**
> Bacteria can even grow on a damp tea towel as even a small amount of moisture is enough to allow growth.

Time

- Given the right conditions, bacteria require time if they are to grow and multiply. A bacterium can split into 2 every 20 minutes or less. In 7 hours the number of bacteria can reach millions.

Oxygen

- Most bacteria require oxygen to grow. These are called **aerobic bacteria**.
- Some do not require oxygen to grow. These are called **anaerobic bacteria**.

> **Top Tip**
> The 'danger zone' is 5–63°C, a range in which bacteria can multiply rapidly.

pH level

- The pH of a substance is a measurement of how acidic or alkaline the substance is and is measured using the pH scale (0–14).
- A pH of 1 or less means the substance is very acidic. A pH of 14 means the substance is very alkaline.
- An acidic pH does not support bacterial growth.
- Most bacteria only grow well at pH 7 which is neither acid nor alkaline.

Food poisoning

Causes of food poisoning

Food poisoning is an illness caused by eating food contaminated with bacteria. Bacteria which can cause food poisoning are called **pathogenic bacteria**. They enter the digestive system when contaminated food is eaten and cause illness.

Symptoms of food poisoning

Symptoms of food poisoning can be mild or severe, and include:

- vomiting
- diarrhoea
- exhaustion
- headache
- fever
- abdominal pain
- tiredness.

If you think you have food poisoning you should not be involved in preparing or handling food. You could pass on the food poisoning bacteria to other people.

Top Tip
Food contaminated with pathogenic bacteria may look, smell and taste normal!

Quick Test

1. List six conditions bacteria need to multiply.
2. At which temperature are most bacteria killed?
3. What is meant by the 'danger zone'?
4. What is the name given to the type of bacteria which can cause food poisoning?
5. List four possible symptoms of food poisoning.

Answers 1. Temperature above 4°C, food, moisture, time, oxygen, acidic pH. **2.** 100°C. **3.** Bacteria can multiply rapidly between 5 – 63°C. **4.** Pathogenic bacteria. **5.** Vomiting, diarrhoea, exhaustion, headache, fever, abdominal pain, tiredness.

Preserving food

Bacterial growth can be prevented by preserving food. This can done in a number of ways. Temperature control, food, moisture, time, oxygen and/or pH level are all used to prevent food from spoiling.

Method of preservation	Description	Suitable foods
Freezing	As temperatures are lowered to -22 to -18°C, bacteria become **dormant** (asleep), so food spoilage is **reduced**. Water changes to ice so there is **less moisture** for bacteria to grow. Bacterial growth increases, however, once food is defrosted.	Meats, poultry, fish, vegetables. Foods can be frozen up to 18 months. Foods with a high water content do not freeze well, e.g. strawberries.
Chilling/ refrigeration	Food is refrigerated at 0–4°C. Bacterial multiplication and food spoilage are **slowed down** but not stopped.	Ready to eat meals, salads, dairy produce, meats.
Jam/ marmalade making	The fruit is boiled to **destroy** enzymes and bacteria (not spores), helping to prevent spoilage. A high concentration of sugar **reduces** bacterial growth and acts as a preservative.	Raspberries, strawberries, oranges, apricots, plums.
Pickling/ chutney making	The ingredients are boiled to **destroy** enzymes and bacteria (not spores), helping to prevent spoilage. The high concentration of acid **prevents** the growth of bacteria (the pH is too acidic).	Many fruits and vegetables can be used to make chutney. Also herring.
Vacuum packaging	Oxygen is removed which **prevents** bacteria multiplying unless they are anaerobic bacteria (do not need oxygen). This method is sometimes used along with chilling, e.g. bacon, so vacuum-packed food often needs to be stored in a refrigerator.	Cold meat, bacon, cheese, fish.
	Modified atmosphere packaging reduces the amount of oxygen inside the pack and increases the carbon dioxide. This means that aerobic bacteria (those needing oxygen) **cannot grow**. The rate of food spoilage slows down.	Ready prepared salads, baked goods, bacon.

Quick Test

1. Name the method of preservation that uses a high concentration of sugar.
2. Name the method of preservation that uses pH.
3. Name the method of preservation that uses a temperature below zero.
4. Name the method of preservation that alters the amount of oxygen but does not remove it altogether.

Answers 1. Jam/marmalade making. 2. Pickling/chutney making. 3. Freezing. 4. Modified atmosphere packaging.

Controlling bacterial growth

Contamination and its prevention

Main causes of food contamination

Food
Raw food may already be contaminated with bacteria so requires correct storage and cooking.

Rubbish
Rubbish contains bacteria which can spread to food. Flies and animals are attracted to rubbish and may also spreead the bacteria to food.

Pets
All animals, including pets and pests, carry bacteria so should not be allowed in food preparation areas.

Top Tip
People can be the main cause of cross-contamination – bacteria found on the body can contaminate food through poor personal hygiene, as can coughing and sneezing.

Cross-contamination

Cross-contamination occurs when bacteria are transferred from one area to another, for example, from raw food to cooked food because of dirty equipment or unhygienic food handling.

All of these rules prevent cross-contamination spreading bacteria:

- Store cooked foods away from raw food.
- In a refrigerator store cooked foods above raw foods (so blood doesn't drip from raw foods).
- Use separate equipment for raw and cooked foods.
- Wash all surfaces and hands thoroughly after preparing raw foods such as chicken.
- Do not use any kitchen utensils, e.g. crockery, that are cracked or chipped.
- Cleaning cloths such as dish towels should be changed daily and disinfected.
- Use disposable cloths if possible.

Preventing contamination by temperature control and cooking food safely

Top Tip
Foods that have been cooked and are to be sold have to be held at a temperature of at least 63°C so that bacteria cannot multiply.

Defrosting
Poultry must be defrosted completely before cooking. If the food is partially frozen, the centre of the food will not reach a high enough temperature during cooking to destroy bacteria.

Cooling
After cooking, food needs to be cooled rapidly, covered and stored in a refrigerator. Food left out in a warm kitchen will be in the danger zone of 5–63°C and bacteria will multiply.

Cooking
The centre of food should reach 75° (core temperature) to ensure bacteria are destroyed.

Reheating
The centre of reheated foods should reach 82°C so bacteria are destroyed. Never reheat food more than once. Do not reheat leftover rice as a bacterium in rice can cause food poisoning.

Buying, transporting and storing food

Consumers have a huge responsibility to play in the prevention of food poisoning through careful buying, transporting and storage of food.

Buying food

Consumer check points	Reason
Check the 'use by' date.	Food must be used by this date as it is no longer safe to eat. Food poisoning could result as bacteria may have multiplied.
Do not buy dented, rusty or blown tins.	Damage to tins may allow oxygen and bacteria to enter and contaminate the food.
Check that foods have been stored below the load line in the deep freeze and are still frozen to touch.	This ensures that the food stays frozen. If food has begun to defrost then bacteria will start to multiply. When refrozen there will be an increased number of bacteria present.
Check packaging for any damage.	Tears or splits in the packaging will allow bacteria and oxygen to enter and contaminate the food.

Top Tip
When shopping check the general cleanliness of the shop and the assistants.

Transportation of food

Consumer check points	Reason
Plan to shop for chilled and frozen foods just before going home.	If chilled and frozen foods are left in a warm car, the temperature of the food will rise and bacteria will start to multiply.
Use an insulated cool bag and freezer blocks; pack frozen and chilled foods together.	To help keep the food cool or prevent frozen food from defrosting. Pack frozen and chilled foods close together to keep them as cold as possible and so prevent bacteria multiplying.
Pack raw and cooked foods separately.	To avoid cross-contamination.
Pack household cleaning materials away from food.	This will prevent the food smelling and tasting of the chemicals or being contaminated by the chemicals.

Storing of food after purchase

Consumer check points	Reason
Unpack and store perishable foods immediately.	Frozen and chilled foods should be stored in chilled conditions immediately to ensure that bacteria cannot multiply.
Check date marks on foods.	Use the FIFO (First In, First Out) system. This ensures no food goes past its expiry date and needs to be thrown out.
Store dry food in a cool, dry, clean place.	This allows the food to remain in the best condition and prevents contamination by pests.

Quick Test

1. List the three main causes of contamination.

2. How many times can food be reheated?

3. Why are raw and cooked foods packed separately?

4. What does FIFO stand for?

Answers 1. Food, rubbish and pets/animals. **2.** Once. **3.** To avoid cross-contamination. **4.** First In, First Out.

Food storage in the home

Food labelling information

Labelling on food packaging plays an important role in preventing food poisoning by ensuring food is stored correctly.

Date marking

The most common date markings are the **Use by** date and the **Best before** date.

Use by
- Used on highly perishable and high risk foods, e.g. meat, yoghurts.
- The food must be used by the date given or there is a risk of food poisoning.
- After purchase these foods could be frozen or cooked – this would extend the 'use by' date.

Best before
- Used on products that are less perishable, e.g. flour, pasta.
- The label means that the product is at its best for quality, flavour and texture before this date.
- Food can be eaten after this date but it may not be at its best for quality, flavour and texture.

Storage

Storage instructions will depend on the **type** of food to be stored.

Non-frozen food

Storage instructions
Empty unused contents into a suitable covered container. Keep refrigerated and use within 2 days.

Storage instructions
Place in a cool dry place. Use within 6 months of opening and before the best before end date.

Storage instructions
Keep refrigerated. Check 'Use by' date.

Frozen food

The **star rating** can be found on all household refrigerators which have an ice-box compartment. The temperature of an **ice-box compartment** is not cold enough to make bacteria dormant – they may be able to multiply slowly. Food can be stored for much longer in a **freezer** because it operates at a much lower temperature of -18°C, ensuring any bacteria are kept dormant.

Storage instructions

Star rating	Storage compartment	Storage times
✳	Frozen food ice-box compartment	1 week after purchase
✳✳	Frozen food ice-box compartment	1 month after purchase
✳✳✳	Frozen food ice-box compartment	3 months after purchase
✳✳✳✳	Food freezer	Long-term storage is possible, depending on the type of food – 3 months or more

⚠ Do not refreeze after thawing – bacterial multiplication will have increased once the product has thawed.

Use of refrigerators and freezers

When the temperature is reduced both food spoilage and bacterial growth are reduced. **Refrigeration** slows down bacterial growth for a **short length of time.**

Freezing at -18°C stops bacterial growth for both **short-** and **long-term storage**.

Some freezers have quick freeze facilities which can reduce the temperature even further, to -24°C. These freeze the food more quickly, so the ice crystals which form within the food are smaller. When food is defrosted there is less damage to the cell structure, so the food keeps its shape better.

Correct temperature

Check the interior temperature with a thermometer. Ensure food is cool before storing – warm or hot food will raise the temperature in the storage compartment and bacteria will multiply. Do not allow warm air to enter the compartment by keeping the door open too long.

Refrigerator – Temperature between 2–4°C.

Freezer – Temperature below -18°C.

Do not overload

Cool air cannot circulate around the food and keep it cool.

Store food correctly

Refrigerator – To prevent cross-contamination:
- raw and cooked should be stored in different areas
- raw food must be stored below cooked foods.

Food should be covered to prevent it from drying out or from absorbing odours.

Freezer – Food should be wrapped well to prevent it drying out and being damaged. Food should be frozen when in its best condition as it will last longer.

Food safety

Refrigerator – Check the 'Use by' date.

Freezer – Food should be clearly labelled and dated so that it is not stored for too long. Do not refreeze defrosted food: as food thaws, the bacteria multiply, and if food is refrozen then there are more bacteria in the food.

Care

Wipe up spills and any food to prevent contamination of other foods. Most refrigerators and freezers are self-defrosting but if not, then defrosting should be done regularly so that the refrigerator or freezer works efficiently and stores food correctly.

Quick Test

1. Name one food which would have a 'Use by' date on it.

2. How should you store left-over tinned peas?

3. What is the correct temperature to store food in a refrigerator?

4. Why should a fridge not be overloaded?

Answers 1. Any highly perishable food, e.g. meat, yoghurts. **2.** Empty unused contents into a suitable covered container, keep refrigerated and use within 2 days. **3.** Between 2–4°C. **4.** Cool air cannot circulate around the food and keep it cool.

Test your progress

Use the questions to test your progress.

1. What is the purpose of the international labelling system for clothes care?

....

2. What do the following laundry symbols mean?

....

3. Explain why cuts should be covered with a blue waterproof plaster when handling food.

....

4. What is food spoilage?

....

5. Explain three ways that enzymes can cause food to deteriorate.

....

6. How are bacteria affected by freezing?

....

7. To what temperature should food be reheated?

....

8. Give a definition of 'high risk' foods.

....

9. Give three examples of high risk foods.

....

10. Give three examples of low risk foods.

....

11. Explain the difference between aerobic and anaerobic bacteria.

....

12. Give a definition of food poisoning.

....

13. Explain the term 'cross-contamination'.

....

14. Why should cooked foods be stored away from raw foods?

....

15. Why should poultry always be thoroughly defrosted?

....

16. How does freezing preserve food?

....

17. How does modified atmosphere packaging slow down the rate of food spoilage?

....

18. When buying foods, why should you always check the packaging for damage?

....

19. a) Name the two most common types of date marks found on food.

....

    b) Explain the difference between them.

....

20. Why should defrosted foods not be refrozen?

....

Answers

1. To ensure clothes are laundered correctly.

2. Wash with minimum agitation and dry flat.

3. Cuts and boils are a breeding ground for bacteria; if the plaster falls off it can be easily seen.

4. Food spoilage is the process that results in food becoming unfit to eat.

5. Ripening – during storage, e.g. bananas go dark brown; browning – certain foods react with the air and discolour, e.g. apples; oxidation – Vitamins A, C and B1 can be lost from food.

6. Bacteria become dormant (or sleepy).

7. 82°C.

8. These foods are called 'perishable foods' as they can 'go off' easily; they usually need to be stored in a refrigerator.

9. Any 3 answers: foods high in protein, e.g. meat, fish; foods high in moisture, e.g. gravies, soups; foods that do not require any further heating, e.g. all cooked meats, poultry and cooked meat products, e.g. pies, sausages; milk, cream, artificial cream, custard and dairy produce; egg products such as mayonnaise; shellfish and sea food; cooked rice.

10. Any 3 answers: foods high in salt, e.g. savoury snacks; foods high in sugar, e.g. jam; foods high in acid, e.g. pickled onions; foods high in fat, e.g. butter, lard; dry foods, e.g. biscuits, cereals.

11. Aerobic bacteria require oxygen to grow, whereas anaerobic bacteria do not require oxygen to grow.

12. It is an illness caused by eating contaminated food.

13. When bacteria are transferred from one area to another.

14. To prevent cross-contamination: bacteria can spread from raw food to cooked food; blood may drip onto cooked foods from raw foods.

15. To ensure that the centre of the food reaches a high enough temperature to destroy bacteria.

16. Food spoilage is reduced as temperatures are lowered to -22 to -18°C; the bacteria become dormant so food spoilage is reduced; water changes to ice so there is less moisture for bacteria to grow.

17. Modified atmosphere packaging reduces the amount of oxygen and increases the carbon dioxide, preventing growth of aerobic bacteria, and slows the rate of food spoilage.

18. Tears or splits in the packaging will allow the entry of bacteria and oxygen and food will become contaminated.

19. a) 'Use by' and 'Best before' b) 'Use by' is used on highly perishable and high risk foods – the food must be used by the date given or there is a risk of food poisoning; 'Best before' is used on products that are less perishable – food can be eaten after this date but it may not be at its best for quality, flavour and texture.

20. As food thaws, bacteria multiply; if food is refrozen then there are more bacteria in the food.

How did you do?

18–20 correct	Excellent	
14–17 correct	Good work	
8–13 correct	Getting there	
1–7 correct	Start again	

Current safe practices 1

Food preparation equipment

Many people are killed or injured due to accidents in the home.

The six main types of accident are:

- cuts
- falls
- electric shock
- poisoning
- burns (from dry heat), e.g. from hot baking trays, matches
- scalds (from moist heat), e.g. from steam, hot water, soup.

There are two groups of people who are most likely to have these accidents:

- **the elderly** because they may have poor co-ordination, eyesight or hearing
- **young children** because they are often curious and less aware of the dangers which can lead to accidents.

The kitchen is usually the most dangerous room in the house as there is a lot of **food preparation equipment**.

Equipment	Rules for safe use
Sharp utensils, e.g. knives, scissors, skewers	To prevent cuts: • store out of the reach of children • store knives in a knife block or locked in drawers • wash blades carefully • do not leave blades soaking in soapy water where they may be forgotten about and accidentally handled.
Cookers – gas and electric	To prevent burns: • young children should not be allowed to play near a cooker – even the cooker sides could cause a burn – or play with the controls of a cooker • use hob guards to prevent young children from getting near the hob of the cooker and pulling hot pans down onto themselves • cookers should be switched off when not in use • use oven gloves when putting dishes into the oven and when removing hot dishes • gas cookers should always be fitted and checked by a registered CORGI gas fitter (see page 73) • if there is a smell of gas and you suspect a possible leak, then contact TRANSCO (emergency gas supplier) immediately • gas cookers should not be fitted beside a window as draughts may blow out the flame; also curtains may catch fire.

Top Tip

If there is a fire while cooking with oil or fat:
- **NEVER** try to move the burning pan (this gives the fire more oxygen and increases the flames)
- **NEVER** throw water over the pan (this will make the fat spit and could cause serious scalds).

Equipment	Rules for safe use
Electrical equipment, e.g. electric mixers, food processors, hand blenders	To prevent electric shocks: • always read the instruction manual before using any new equipment • never touch any plugs, sockets or electrical equipment with wet hands • always ensure equipment is unplugged before assembling or disassembling • switch off at the mains supply before and after use • never put electrical equipment into water – wipe it with a damp soapy cloth and dry. • don't use if flex is damaged
Microwave ovens	To prevent accidents: • have your microwave tested annually for leakage by a professional • do not put any metal dishes in a microwave oven • microwave containers and their contents become extremely hot – use oven gloves when removing items from the oven • use only non-PVC cling film as this is safe to use in a microwave • when peeling off any cling film covering a dish, peel it off towards you so the steam escapes away from you • do not use any fats and oils in microwave cooking as they can overheat easily.

One of the main causes of accidents in the home – causing scalds as well as house fires – involves cooking with fats and oils.

Rules for cooking safely with fats and oils

• Fats and oils can reach very high temperatures during frying. Electrical equipment (deep fat fryer or frying pan) are safer than using a chip pan on the cooker because they cut off automatically when the correct temperature has been reached, so there is less risk of over heating and fire.

• Never leave a hot pan of fat or oil unattended.

• If there is a fire: keep calm, switch off the heat, cover the pan with a damp cloth or a tight fitting lid to exclude the oxygen, and leave the pan to cool down.

Quick Test

1. Name two groups of people who are at most risk from household accidents.

2. If there is a hot fat fire, what four actions should you take?

3. What is the first action you should take before using any new electrical equipment?

Answers 1. The elderly and young children. 2. Keep calm, switch off, cover pan with a damp cloth/tight fitting lid and leave pan to cool. 3. Read the instruction manual.

Current safe practices 2

Care of clothing

It is important to use laundering equipment (e.g. washing machines, tumble driers, ironing equipment) safely when caring for clothes

Equipment	Rules for safe use
Washing machine	• Ensure young children do not tamper with any controls or are near the washing machine when it is operating. • Always ensure that any safety lock features of the machine door are working. This applies to front or top loading washing machines. • Do not leave any detergents or laundry products where children could tamper or play with them.
Tumble drier	• Always ensure the safety lock features of the drier door are working. • Ensure that young children stay away from the drier when it is in use so that they don't burn or scald themselves. • Small children should not be allowed to climb into a tumbler drier (even when it is not being used) as a faulty door catch could trap the child inside.
Iron	• Read manufacturer's instructions before use. • Check the flex is not bare at any place and is free from tangles. • Never leave a hot iron unattended. • When filling a steam iron with water, ensure that the iron is unplugged. • Always have the iron at the correct temperature setting for the fabric being used. • Rest the iron on its heel between ironing garments. • After use, leave the iron to cool in safe place out of the reach of young children.
Ironing board	• Ensure the ironing board is correctly set up, level and standing firmly. • The ironing board cover should be securely fixed and any ties tucked away. • Never leave an ironing board unattended if there are young children around. • Store the ironing board in a safe place where it cannot fall over.

Top Tip
Before using all electrical laundering equipment, remember to read the instruction manual carefully.

Use of sewing equipment

When using sewing equipment, either at home or in school, the following safety rules must be followed.

Equipment	Rules for safe use
Sewing machine	• Read the instruction manual before using the machine. In school your teacher will demonstrate how to use it. • For safety, complete concentration is required, so only one person at a time should be using the sewing machine. • Always ensure long hair, loose clothing and hands are away from the needle when using the sewing machine. • Check the flex for any signs of damage. • Sewing machines are heavy so be careful when lifting. • Maintain and service the sewing machine regularly.
Pins and needles 	• Keep pins and needles safe in a container with a tight fitting lid or in a locked cupboard. • Pick up immediately any pins and needles that fall to the ground. • Always check you haven't left pins or needles lying around when you finish sewing. • Never play with/hold pins or needles in your mouth while working.
Scissors	• Always use the best quality scissors as they will be sharper, and so safer, for cutting thick fabrics but be careful of where your fingers are placed when cutting as the blades are dangerous. • Keep all types of scissors in a firmly closed container or in a locked cupboard out of the reach of children. • When carrying scissors always hold them by the closed blades. • When you pass scissors to someone hold them by the blade with the handle towards the person.

Quick Test

1. Which safety feature do washing machines and tumble driers have in common?
2. What type of accident could happen if a child touched a tumble drier while it is operating?
3. How should scissors be handed to another person?
4. To ensure you are using the sewing machine safely, what should not be near the needle when working?

Answers 1. Safety lock feature. **2.** Burn or scald. **3.** Hold them by the blade and give the handle to the person. **4.** Long hair, hands and loose clothing.

Safety around the home

Top Tip
In an exam question on accidents in the home you may be asked to describe:
• cause of accident or possible hazard
• type of accident which would happen as a result
• relevant safety rules or action to prevent the accident.

Accidents can happen in different areas in the home. The following charts list some of the hazards which are likely in each area, the type of accident and how to prevent them.

Area of the home: KITCHEN

Cause or hazard	Type of accident	How to prevent an accident
Frayed flex on electrical items	Electric shock	Do not use until the flex has been replaced.
Using a stool or chair to reach a high cupboard or shelf	Fall	A secure step ladder should be used as stools and chairs are unsteady.
Saucepan on the cooker hob with the pan handle sticking out	Scald	Always have saucepan handles turned to the side or the back of the cooker. Fit a cooker guard to the hob.
Removing dishes from oven or microwave using a cloth	Burn	Use thick oven gloves to prevent the heat going through to your hands.
Sharp utensils, e.g. knives, tins, broken glass and crockery	Cuts	Always store safely, out of the reach of children. Wrap broken items in thick newspaper and dispose of safely.
Cleaning fluids, some foods/drinks	Poisoning	All cleaning chemicals should be stored carefully. Food/drink which may cause problems should be stored away from the reach of children.

Area of the home: BATHROOM

Cause or hazard	Type of accident	How to prevent an accident
Using electrical equipment with wet hands or in a wet area	Electric shock	Do not use electrical equipment in the bathroom or with wet hands.
Water is too hot straight from the tap	Scald	Always mix hot and cold water together before filling the bath.
Slippery surface on bath or shower floor	Fall	Use a non-slip mat in bath or shower.
Medicines, cleaning chemicals	Poisoning	All medicines and chemicals should be kept in a special cabinet out of the reach of children.

Top Tip
Some of these hazards are found in more than one area of the house, e.g. frayed flexes could be found on electrical equipment used in a number of areas.

Area of the home: LIVING ROOM

Cause or hazard	Type of accident	How to prevent an accident
Open coal fire or gas fire	Burn	Always use a fire guard which is fixed to the wall in front of a fire.
Matches, lighter left around	Burn	Store in a safe place.
Hot drinks, teapots sitting on tables	Scald	Do not leave hot cups of tea, coffee on low tables especially if children are around. Be careful if using a tablecloth as a child could pull this and spill hot drinks.
Overloaded electric sockets	Electric shock	Never overload power sockets – take some plugs out. Always switch off sockets and unplug after use.
Child sticking fingers or an object into an electric socket	Electric shock	Use electric socket guards when there are children around.
Rug placed on a polished floor	Fall	Always firmly secure rugs or do not place them on polished floors.
Objects lying around the floor (e.g. toys, books, flexes)	Fall	Keep the floor space clear. Do not have flexes trailing across floors.

Area of the home: HALL and STAIR

Cause or hazard	Type of accident	How to prevent an accident
Hall or stairs dimly lit	Fall	These areas must be well lit to ensure safety, particularly for elderly people.
Babies or young children climbing stairs	Fall	Use a safety gate to prevent young children from climbing up or down stairs.

Area of the home: GARDEN

Cause or hazard	Type of accident	How to prevent an accident
Chemicals, flammable or poisonous materials left lying around	Poisoning, burns	Store these materials in a safe place. Never store chemicals in unmarked soft drink bottles.
Electric mowers/strimmers	Electric shock, cuts	Keep flexes out of the way when using these pieces of equipment. Switch off and unplug electric equipment when emptying and cleaning.
Sharp equipment (e.g. garden scissors, rake, shovel)	Cuts	Store carefully and securely.

Quick Test

1. What is the difference between a burn and a scald?
2. What would you do with broken glass in the kitchen?
3. Name two safety devices which could prevent a child having an accident in the home.

Answers 1. A burn is caused by dry heat, a scald by moist heat. **2.** Wrap in thick newspaper and dispose of safely. **3.** Cooker guard, safety gate, electric socket guards.

Test your progress

Use the questions to test your progress.

1. Explain why the elderly can be more at risk from accidents in the home than other age groups. . . . .

2. Why are children often the victims of accidents in the home? . . . .

3. Name the six main types of accident which can happen in the home. . . . .

4. List five pieces of food preparation equipment where an accident can happen if care is not taken. . . . .

5. Where should sharp kitchen knives be stored? . . . .

6. What two accidents could happen if a gas cooker is fitted too near a window? . . . .

7. Give two safety rules to follow when using electrical equipment. . . . .

8. Give two safety rules to follow when using a microwave for heating foods. . . . .

9. Why are electrical deep fat fryers safer to use than heating oil in a saucepan on a hob? . . . .

10. What two actions must you never take if a fat or oil fire occurs? . . . .

11. List two precautions to take to ensure safe use of an iron. . . . .

12. State three safety rules for using the sewing machine. . . . .

13. Give three rules for the safe use of scissors. . . . .

14. a) Identify two types of accident which could happen when using a hand blender. . . . .

   b) Explain how each of these accidents could have been prevented. . . . .

15. State two ways to avoid burns and scalds in the kitchen. . . . .

16. What is the safest way of reaching for an item in a high cupboard? . . . .

17. Where should medicines be stored in a bathroom? . . . .

18. Give two rules to follow to ensure that the halls and stairs are safe for an elderly person. . . . .

19. Explain two ways that a living room could be made safer for a toddler. . . . .

20. a) Safe floors are essential in the home to prevent falls. State three hazards which could cause a fall. . . . .
    b) Describe how each of these hazards could be prevented. . . . .

21. State one rule to follow to ensure safe use of an electric lawn mower when cutting the grass. . . . .

Answers

1. Because they may have poor coordination, eyesight or hearing.

2. Because they are often curious and less aware of the dangers which can lead to accidents.

3. Cuts, falls, electric shock, poisoning, burns and scalds.

4. Sharp utensils, cookers, electrical equipment, microwave ovens, pans of fat.

5. In a knife block or locked drawer.

6. Draughts could blow out the flame or curtains could catch fire.

7. Any 2 answers: always read the instruction manual before using any new equipment; never touch any plugs, sockets or electrical equipment with wet hands; always ensure equipment is unplugged before assembling or disassembling; switch off at the mains supply before and after use; never put electrical equipment into water – wipe with a damp soapy cloth and dry.

8. Any 2 answers: test annually for microwave leakage; do not put any metal dishes in microwave oven; microwave containers and their contents become extremely hot – remove from the oven using oven gloves; use only non-PVC cling film as this is safe to use in a microwave; when peeling off any cling film covering a dish, peel it off towards you so the steam escapes away from you; do not use any fats or oils in microwave cooking as they can overheat easily.

9. They cut off automatically when the correct temperature has been reached, so there is less risk of overheating.

10. Do not move the burning pan (this gives the fire more oxygen and increases the flames); do not throw water over the pan (this will make the fat spit and could cause serious scalds).

11. Any 2 answers: check the flex is not bare at any place and is free from tangles; never leave a hot iron unattended; when filling a steam iron with water, ensure that the iron is unplugged; always have the iron at the correct temperature setting for the fabric being used; after use, leave the iron to cool in safe place out of the reach of young children.

12. Read the instruction manual before using; only one person at a time should be using the sewing machine; always ensure long hair, loose clothing and hands are not near the needle when using the sewing machine.

13. Ensure scissors are sharp so they are safer for cutting thick fabrics; take care where your fingers are placed when cutting as the blades are dangerous; when carrying scissors always hold them by the closed blades; when you pass scissors to someone hold them by the blade with the handle towards the person.

14. a) Electric shock, cuts, scalds; b) Read instructions before use; switch on using dry hands; take care when using to prevent hot splashes; switch off power after use; do not clean or remove attachments when power is switched on; do not use if flex is damaged; do not immerse in water when cleaning.

15. Keep pan handles turned in the way; use oven gloves when removing dishes from the oven; use a cooker guard on the hob.

16. A secure step ladder.

17. In a special cabinet out of the reach of children.

18. Ensure the area is well lit; do not leave objects lying around on the stairs, e.g. toys.

19. Any 2 answers: use a fire guard; do not leave lighters or matches lying around; do not have hot drinks/teapots sitting on low tables; do not use tablecloths; use electric socket guards; do not polish under rugs; do not leave objects lying around; do not have trailing flexes.

20. a) Any 3 answers: spills, polished floor under rugs, trailing flexes, toys or other objects lying around; b) Any 3 answers relating to part a): wipe up spills immediately; do not polish under rugs; shorten the flex or use a nearer socket; tidy up objects left on the floor.

21. Keep the flex out of the way.

How did you do?

1–7 correct	Start again	8–13 correct	Getting there
14–18 correct	Good work	19–21 correct	Excellent

Influences on choice of materials and equipment

Factors that influence choices

Before we buy any item there are a number of factors that will influence our choice. The item could be:

- food
- clothing } **materials**
- footwear

- food preparation equipment (e.g. knives, food processor)
- basic sewing equipment (e.g. scissors, sewing machine) } **equipment**
- white goods (e.g. washing machine, cooker, refrigerator)

Before we buy any of these items we will be influenced by a number of factors.

Top Tip

In the exam you may be given a case study with a target group and then asked to say which design features are suitable for that target group.

Income

More income means a greater choice or, often, access to a better quality item. Less income may mean less choice or access to a poorer quality item. If you have a limited income you may have to prioritise and decide if a purchase is absolutely necessary.

What you already own

This will affect what you still need to buy and also if you need to match an existing item, e.g. matching colours of an outfit or home décor.

Advertising

Advertisements are targeted at particular groups of people and may influence them to buy items that they do not really need or choose some instead of others.

Availability/Access

Where you stay will affect the range of items you can buy. People who live in towns and cities may have a larger choice of items than people who live in villages or in the countryside. However, other purchasing options are available to most people (and increase the range of what they can buy), no matter where they live: over the internet, by mail order, through TV shopping channels.

The size of the item

This applies to such items as white goods that may have to fit into a certain area in the kitchen – this may limit choice.

Method of payment

Methods of payment may affect what you can buy. Choice of items may be restricted by whether you want to pay cash or use credit or interest-free credit.

Influences on choice of materials and equipment

Before finally choosing an item, it is important to consider and compare the **design features** of the choices that are available. Design features could relate to food, equipment or fabrics. You need to think about which features make the item most suitable for its purpose.

Look at the design features of a school sweatshirt indicated here.

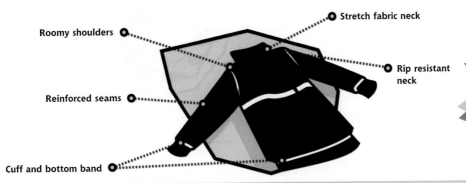

Roomy shoulders

Stretch fabric neck

Rip resistant neck

Reinforced seams

Cuff and bottom band

Top Tip
Some of the areas of design can overlap depending on the design feature (see page 58).

Design areas and design features

There are six design areas to consider when designing a product. The design features of any product will always be linked to these design areas.

1 Materials
- These should be suitable for the item, e.g. waterproof fabric for an outdoor jacket
- Ease/cost of cleaning

2 Construction
- The construction should give strength to allow the item to be used
- Construction should make the item stable during use, e.g. a food processor

3 Performance
- The item should perform its function/purpose, e.g. a chopping board should withstand continual chopping

DESIGN

6 Aesthetic/Personal
- Appearance: does it look good, is the colour appropriate, is it fashionable?
- Personal likes and dislikes
- Family/peer group opinion and pressures, e.g. responding to advertisinng
- Personal/family beliefs and values, e.g. environmental factors (recycling), religious issues (modesty of clothing)

5 Safety
- Materials and construction should make the item safe, stable and hygienic to use, e.g. reflective strips on outerwear for cycling at night
- Ease and safety when using, cleaning, assembling and storing

4 Durability
- The item should last for a reasonable length of time so that you get value for money

On the next pages we will look at two products – one food, one fabric item – in relation to these six design areas.

Quick Test

1. Explain why a rip resistant neck would be an important design feature if you were choosing this sweatshirt to wear to school.

2. List the six areas of design to be considered.

3. Why is durability important?

Design areas

Product 1: healthy eating individual pasta snack

The table below shows how the six different design areas need to be considered in the design of a healthy pasta snack for one person, resulting in specific design features.

Design area	Design features
Materials	
The packaging should:	• be made from strong materials to protect and preserve the product • not affect the taste of the product.
The ingredients should:	• contribute to a healthy diet • not be affected by storage or packaging, e.g. no discolouring.
Construction	
The packaging should:	• be strong enough to protect the product • be tamper-proof to prevent contamination • be large enough to contain the product and be easy to hold • allow contents to be seen • allow the product to be eaten immediately.
The ingredients should:	• look good and combine well together.
Performance	
The product should:	• be ready to eat • be easy to open and eat • contain ingredients which contribute to a healthy diet.
Safety	
The product should:	• have tamper proof packaging to prevent contamination • have no sharp edges to cause cuts • have clear storage instructions with a 'use by' date.
Durability	
The product should:	• be able to withstand transportation during delivery and after purchase • have a 'use by' date that allows an acceptable length of storage time.
Aesthetic/personal	
The packaging should:	• be eye-catching to encourage purchase • be the appropriate colour for the type of product.
The product should:	• be attractive to encourage consumption • contain ingredients that appeal to consumers.

Top Tip

Have you noticed how some of the design areas of the pasta snack overlap?

Product 2: any item made of fabric

When designing a fabric item, you need to consider the purpose or function of the item and how this can be achieved by the **properties** (or qualities) of the different fibres used to make the fabric. These properties are highlighted in the table below. See pages 64–65 for more information on the properties of fabrics.

Fabric property **required by design area**	Appropriate fibres/fabrics
Materials	
Water repellent – water is not absorbed by fabric so the wearer is kept dry, e.g. hill walking jacket	microfibres, microporous membranes
Warmth/insulation – to keep wearer warm, e.g. winter coat	wool, acrylic 'fleece'
Construction	
Strength – a strong fabric and sturdy seams would be required for a workman's outfit	heavy-duty cotton, linen, nylon
Elasticity – used to allow stretch and movement, e.g. sportswear	cotton, polyester, nylon, elastane
Performance	
Breathability – allows moisture (e.g. perspiration) to escape but also stops water from getting in	microfibres, microporous membranes
Ease of laundering – frequent use means machine-washable fabrics are most suitable	cotton, polyester
Absorbency – absorbs moisture so helps keep the wearer dry, e.g. a sports T-shirt	cotton, linen, silk, wool, viscose
Stain resistance – the fabric resists stains and is easier to clean, e.g. carpets	wool and acrylic can be treated with a stain-resistant finish
Elasticity – again, allowing stretch and movement, e.g. cycling shorts	cotton, polyester, nylon, elastane
Crease resistance – the ability of the fabric to resist creasing may be important when laundering and wearing	wool, acrylic, polyester, elastane
Safety	
Flammability – by law, some items must be made of fabrics that are flame resistant, e.g. children's nightwear	wool, cotton, silk, linen
Warmth/insulation – elderly people need to be kept warm in order to maintain body temperature; insulation is important for oven gloves	wool, acrylic
Durability	
Strength – the stronger the fabric the longer it will last	linen, polyester, nylon, elastane
Durability – the fabric must be hardwearing especially if washed a lot	cotton, linen, silk, nylon, polyester, elastane
Aesthetic/personal	
Crease resistant – clothes look smarter if they do not crease when worn	wool, acrylic, polyester, elastane

These thermal gloves require the properties of: warmth, strength, durability, absorbency, water repellence and elasticity.

Warmth • Strength • Absorbency • Water repellence • Elasticity • Durability

Quick Test

1. Why should packaging be tamper proof?

2. What is the benefit of stain resistant fabric?

3. Why is elasticity an important property for cycling shorts?

Answers 1. To prevent contamination. 2. It is easier to clean. 3. Fabric stretches so allows movement.

Conservation of resources

Conserving energy and reducing running costs

Conserving or saving energy means trying to reduce the amount of energy (gas, oil and electricity) we use. We can do this by being careful when using electrical and other equipment, and also by choosing energy-efficient equipment.

Ways to reduce energy use around the home

Insulate the home

All of these measures reduce heat loss throughout the house and so will lower the cost of heating:

- install double-glazed windows
- install thick curtains
- have well fitting doors and windows
- have carpets instead of bare floorboards
- install loft and cavity wall insulation
- insulate the hot water tank and pipes.

Reduce the amount of energy used

All of these measures reduce the amount of energy used and so will lower fuel bills:

- lower the heating thermostat by 1°C
- have a shower instead of a bath
- use energy saving light bulbs
- do not leave electrical equipment, e.g. TV, on standby. Always switch off and unplug
- only boil the required amount of water in the kettle
- washing machines and dishwashers should have a full load, or use an economy programme if not a full load.

Top Tip

Design features are often presented as part of a case study in Handling Information questions. Advances in design features are happening all the time – these are usually explained for you in some part of the question. But you must also link these to the case study.

Choosing energy-efficient electrical equipment

Design features

The following are some **design features** of electrical equipment which will enable you to choose energy efficient equipment.

Cooker	Tumble drier	Washing machine
• Different size of rings or burners to suit different pan sizes.	• Variable heat settings for different fabrics.	• Half load or economy wash for small loads uses less water.
• Fan ovens reduce cooking time.	• Sensor dry feature – when clothes are dry the tumble drier stops.	• Quick wash cycle – shorter wash time.
• Half-width grilling facilities for small portions.	• Ecosensor – automatically switches to a cool cycle when clothes are dry.	• High spin speed leaves washing drier so saves tumble drying time.
• Top ovens can be used for smaller portions.	• Reverse tumble dry – dries more quickly.	• Automatic water level control – adjusts amount of water to wash load.

Energy ratings

The Energy Labelling Directive requires that appliances be labelled to show how much energy they use. This allows consumers to compare the energy efficiency of similar products, helping consumers choose the most energy efficient product.

The Directive applies to:

- washing machines
- tumble driers
- combined washer-driers
- refrigerators
- freezers
- dishwashers
- light bulbs.

Products are rated on a 7-point scale according to how much energy they use:

most energy efficient   *least energy efficient*

  A   B   C   D   E   F   G

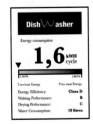

In addition, many appliance labels give a more detailed breakdown, for example:

Recycling

Recycling is the process of recovering and reusing waste products and so reducing damage to the environment. Products which have been or can be recycled may encourage consumers to purchase them.

Ways to recycle household items

- Textile items can be:
  — taken to a recycling centre where they can be made into new fabrics
  — taken to a charity shop for reselling or donation to overseas charities.
- Glass, paper, steel, aluminium and plastics can all be taken to 'banks' where they will be collected and recycled.
- Food waste can be used for garden compost.

Quick Test

1. How can you prevent heat being lost through windows?
2. State two design features that a cooker may have which would save energy.
3. Name two products that may have an energy rating on the label.

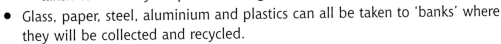

Answers 1. Double-glazed windows, or by having thick curtains. **2.** Different size of rings or burners; fan ovens; half-width grilling facilities or top ovens. **3.** Washing machines; tumble driers; combined washer-driers; refrigerators; freezers; dishwashers; light bulbs.

Test your progress

Use the questions to test your progress.

1. Name two items of white goods. ....
....

2. List three factors which can influence purchase of white goods. ....
....

3. Why are design features important? ....
....

4. A bag to carry your books to school should have the following design feature: a strong
padded handle. Give two reasons for this. ....
....

5. A saucepan must have following design feature: heat resistant handles. Give one reason
for this. ....
....

6. List two safety design features to consider when choosing a food processor. ....
....

7. Why should items be durable? ....
....

8. Give one reason why food packaging should be strong. ....
....

9. Why would warmth be an important property for an elderly person's clothes? ....
....

10. State two properties that children's nightwear should have. ....
....

11. Why would a combination of wool and nylon be good when manufacturing socks? ....
....

12. What does the phrase 'conserving energy in the home' mean? ....
....

13. Apart from windows, what other areas in the home can be insulated to prevent heat loss?
....

14. State two ways to save fuel bills. ....
....

15. Explain two energy saving features that a tumble drier may have. ....
....

16. What is the advantage to the consumer of the energy rating system being shown on a
product's label? ....
....

17. Explain the term 'recycling'. ....
....

18. How can textile items be recycled? ....
....

19. How can food waste be used? ....
....

20. What do the following two symbols mean?

a) .... b)

How did you do?

18–20 correct	Excellent
14–17 correct	Good work
8–13 correct	Getting there
1–7 correct	Start again

Answers

1. Any 2 answers: washing machine, cooker, tumble drier, refrigerator, freezer.

2. Any 3 answers: income, what is already owned, advertising, availability, size and method of payment.

3. Because they must meet the needs of the target group.

4. It must be: strong as school books are heavy; padded so that it is more comfortable to carry and does not rub against the hand.

5. So hands and fingers do not get burnt when lifting the pan.

6. Any 2 answers: it must be stable, made of safe materials, safe to use, easy to use.

7. So that they last a reasonable length of time and give value for money.

8. Any 1 answer: to protect and preserve the food; to withstand transportation.

9. To help maintain the elderly person's body heat (and prevent hypothermia).

10. Any 2 answers: ease of laundering, non-flammability, absorbency.

11. The wool gives warmth and the nylon gives strength.

12. Trying to reduce the amount of energy used and choosing electrical equipment that uses energy efficiently and which has low running costs.

13. Doors, lofts, walls, hot water tanks and pipes.

14. Any 2 answers: lower the heating thermostat by 1°C; have a shower instead of a bath; do not leave electrical equipment on standby; turn off equipment completely when not in use; use energy saving light bulbs; washing machines and dishwashers should have a full load or use an economy programme.

15. Any 2 answers: variable heat settings for different fabrics saves energy costs; sensor dry feature – when clothes are dry the tumble drier stops; ecosensor – automatically switches to a cool cycle when clothes are dry to save energy; reverse tumble dry – dries clothes more quickly so saves energy.

16. Consumers who prefer energy efficient products can compare similar products and choose the most suitable one.

17. Recycling is the process of recovering and reusing waste products and so reducing damage to the environment.

18. They can be taken to a recycling centre where they can be made into new fabrics, or taken to a charity shop for reselling or donation to overseas charities.

19. For garden compost.

20. a) Recycled material has been used for packaging; b) This glass is recyclable – please put this in a bottle bank.

Clothing 1

We wear clothing for a number of reasons: to give **protection**, for **comfort**, for **safety**, to give a particular **impression**, and to give **identity**.

The properties of textiles used in clothing and footwear need to be considered when assessing whether items will satisfy our needs.

Protection

Textiles can keep us **warm**, **cool** and **dry**. They also give us privacy.

Warm	To keep warm we must insulate our bodies from the cold by trapping air inside our clothing. This can be achieved in a number of ways:

- wearing a number of thin layers of clothing
- some fabrics trap air and are naturally warm, e.g. wool
- some fabrics are constructed to trap air, e.g. knitted, quilted and fleece garments.

Cool	• When we are active we perspire. Some fabrics, e.g. cotton, absorb perspiration (and then release it through evaporation) and so help to keep the body dry and cool. • Wearing lighter weight clothing when the weather is hot can keep us cool.
Dry	**Breathable** fabrics, such as tightly woven **microfibres** and those treated with **microporous membranes**, keep us dry because they prevent moisture penetrating the fabric but allow perspiration to escape.

Design features: garments with specific design features will also keep you warm, cool and dry, e.g. elasticated cuffs, concealed front zip with Velcro closing tab.

Comfort

The following factors affect the **comfort** or **fit** of our clothes.

Size	If clothes are too tight, we may feel uncomfortable. Some fabrics are produced with **elastomeric** fibres which can stretch and feel more comfortable, e.g. jeans.
Weight	If a garment feels heavy, it may be uncomfortable to wear.
Absorbency	Fabrics which can absorb moisture (perspiration) and allow that moisture to evaporate, e.g. cotton polo shirt, will be more comfortable than a fabric that stays wet and clingy.
Elasticity	The clothes we wear should allow us to move freely. Certain garments, e.g. sportswear, need to allow a lot of movement.
Softness	The feel of fabric next to your skin contributes to a garment's comfort.
Crease resistance	Many synthetic fabrics have crease-resistant finishes to improve the comfort and appearance of clothes.
Fastenings	The type of fastening should be appropriate to the wearer and the purpose of the garment.

Safety

Aspects of clothing which concern safety include the **type** of fabric, its **colour** and the type of **fastenings**.

Type of fabric
- Fabrics offer general protection from sharp objects, while some clothing protects from specific dangers, e.g. firefighter's uniforms.
- Fabrics can be treated to make them flame resistant (non-flammable), so they will not easily catch fire near a naked flame, e.g. child's nightwear.
- Fabrics which trap air tend to be more **inflammable** (likely to catch fire), e.g. knitted garments.
- Fabrics can be coated with PVC (polyvinyl chloride), making them safer when used near boiling liquid, e.g. aprons.

Colour
- Some garments are made in extremely bright (high visibility) colours to make sure the wearer is easily seen. Reflective strips ensure the wearer is visible at night.

Fastenings
- Children's garments require secure fastenings to prevent accidents, e.g. choking on buttons.

Impression and appearance

Wearing the latest fashion is more important for some people than it is for others. But no matter what clothing we wear, we want it to make us look and feel good. It may be for work, leisure or a special occasion, e.g. a wedding. Because we are all different ages, shapes and sizes, and have different ideas of what looks good and what is important, our choices will be different. Designers work hard to meet these different choices.

Identity

Our clothing may show that we belong to a specific group or occupation, e.g. school uniform, doctor's white coat. Our choice of clothing and style of appearance may also show, in an informal way, that we belong to a certain group.

Footwear

Consider the following aspects when choosing footwear:
- size and width fittings to ensure comfort
- structure to ensure correct future bone formation
- support to carry weight of the body and to protect the feet.

Quick Test

1. Give three reasons why we wear clothing.
2. What properties do textiles have which can give us protection?
3. What type of fabric should be used to make children's nightwear?

Answers 1. To give protection, comfort, safety, be attractive and give identity. **2.** They can keep us warm, cool and dry. **3.** Flame resistant/non-flammable.

Clothing 2

Clothing requirements of groups of individuals

The following groups have particular needs for clothing and footwear. The purpose of clothing, its cost in relation to use, and the occasion when it is to be worn will influence choice.

Babies and toddlers

Requirement	Reason
Comfort and softness	● Fabric should be soft to prevent rubbing of delicate skin. ● There should be no tight elastic, thick seams or zips.
Durability	● To withstand being washed often. ● To withstand stretching during dressing and general wear and tear.
Stretch	● To allow movement and play. ● Makes it easier to dress and undress.
Ease of laundering	● Clothes need to be quick to wash and dry. ● Non-iron/crease-resistant fabrics save time ironing.
Safety	● Avoid ribbons which can tangle fingers. ● Buttons need to be securely fastened. ● Clothes should not be too baggy or long. ● No sharp buckles and buttons.
Absorbency	● To absorb perspiration.
Temperature control	● Babies find it difficult to control body temperature so it is better to dress them in several layers of thin clothing which can be added to or removed in order to help maintain body temperature. ● Outdoor clothing for toddlers should be warm and waterproof to protect against the weather.
Footwear	● When they start walking babies must have their feet measured to ensure a good fit and support. ● Toddlers' footwear and socks should fit well and allow for some room for growth. Velcro fastenings encourage independence.

Adolescents (teenagers)/adults

Requirement	Reason
Comfort	● Fabric should be comfortable to wear. ● Stretchy if the clothing is to be used in active pursuits.
Ease of laundering	● Clothing may be a favourite item and so may be worn often, so the fabric should be easy to wash, dry and iron. ● Avoid clothes that need (expensive) dry cleaning.
Absorbency	● To absorb perspiration if wearer is active.
Temperature control	● Clothing should allow wearer to be warm or cool, depending on the occasion/climate/activity.
Footwear	● Footwear should fit well as some fashion shoes may cause foot problems.

Top Tip
Nightwear for **all groups** must be non-flammable for safety.

Elderly/people with physical disabilities

The type of disability a person has affects their clothing and footwear requirements, e.g. the needs of a person who has limited hand use will be different from a person with limited sight.

Requirement	Reason
Comfort: softness, stretch and absorbency	● The elderly/physically disabled may be bed bound so comfort is important. ● Fabric should be soft to prevent skin irritation. ● Clothing should not be tight. ● Stretch allows movement and makes it easier to dress. ● Fabric should absorb perspiration.
Ease of laundering	● Quick to wash and dry. Easy-care items are important for people who lack mobility or strength. ● Crease-resistant or non-iron fabrics save effort.
Safety	● Clothing should not be too long.
Temperature control	● The elderly find it difficult to control body temperature so wearing several layers of thin clothing which can be easily added to or removed helps maintain a comfortable body temperature. ● The elderly and physically disabled may have poorer circulation and so feel the cold more, leading, in extreme situations, to hypothermia.
Ease of fastening	● Fastenings should be easy to handle, especially if there are problems with agility, e.g. difficulty fastening buttons. ● Elasticated waistbands make dressing easier. ● Front fastenings are easier to reach than back fastenings.
Footwear	● Shoes should have non-slip soles, be well fitting, comfortable and give support. Slip-on shoes or shoes with Velcro fastenings may be better than lace-ups.

Pregnant women

Requirement	Reason
Comfort: softness, stretch	● Clothing should be loose fitting to allow for comfort, movement and growth. Fabrics should be soft and stretchy to allow for an increase in body size.
Ease of laundering	● Clothes should be quick to wash and dry as the woman may not have many clothes to choose from. ● Crease-resistant or non-iron fabrics save effort.
Safety	● Clothing should not be too long or baggy.
Ease of fastening	● Fastenings should be adjustable to accommodate increasing body size. Front fastenings will be easier to reach than back fastenings.
Footwear	● Shoes should provide support and shoe width will have to cope with swollen feet. ● Flat or low heels are more comfortable and safer than high heels.

Quick Test

1. Why must clothing for babies be able to stretch?

2. Why should teenagers not choose clothes which require dry cleaning?

3. What kind of footwear is advisable for elderly people?

Answers 1. To allow movement and make it easier for dressing. 2. Because dry cleaning is expensive. 3. Shoes with non-slip soles, that fit well, give support: slip-on or with Velcro fastenings.

Shelter

Types and importance

Shelter is required by individuals and families to give:

- protection from the weather
- safety and security
- privacy
- a place to rest and sleep
- warmth from gas, electricity or oil
- water for drinking and washing
- toilet facilities.

The type of shelter required will depend on your stage of life, your age and health, the number in the family or the combination of people living together. The following table describes a variety of accommodation suitable for different groups.

Accommodation	Explanation
Flats, houses (detached, semi-detached, bungalow)	This type of accommodation can be either privately owned or rented from the local authority, housing associations or private landlords. When buying accommodation you must ensure you have sufficient money to pay the deposit and the mortgage. Renting may be more suitable if you intend to move frequently.
Student accommodation	Students may share a flat or house, rent a room within a private house, or use halls of residence.
Homes linked to jobs	Some jobs provide accommodation, e.g. army, RAF. If you leave the job, however, you lose your home.
Temporary accommodation	Sometimes accommodation is required for a short term, e.g when waiting for a new home.
Caravans and mobile homes	For some people these may be permanent or temporary.
Sheltered housing	When an elderly or disabled person is unable to live on their own this type of supervised accommodation allows them some independence.

Top Tip

When answering an exam question about accommodation, always consider the likely reasons why people live in such accommodation, e.g. an elderly person would be more suited to live in a bungalow or ground floor flat as there are no stairs.

Quick Test

1. Give four reasons why we need shelter.
2. State two factors which could affect the type of housing chosen.
3. Why is sheltered housing suitable for an elderly person who finds it difficult to live on their own?

Well-being

Physical factors which contribute to good health and general well-being include: a well balanced diet (see page 8), personal cleanliness (see page 36), adequate sleep, fresh air and exercise, and general good habits.

Sleep

- While we sleep our bodies are still functioning and self-repairing.
- The older we are the less sleep we need. Adults should have 6–8 hours, whereas babies sleep much more.
- Our state of health, our occupation, how active we are and the climate we live in also affect how much sleep we need.

Top Tip
How to get a good night's sleep:
- don't eat fatty or filling foods before going to bed
- try to relax before going to bed.

Fresh air and exercise

Fresh air has more oxygen so will help you feel more alert. All forms of exercise offer these benefits:

- it tones the muscles, making the heart and lungs more efficient
- it aids sleep and appetite
- improves bone density
- it helps reduce stress and makes you feel good
- it uses energy and helps weight control.

Top Tip
When pregnant, smoking and alcohol are not advised as the baby may be harmed

Good habits

It is important not to damage our bodies by using harmful substances. Addiction to any sort of drug can affect health, ability to work, and personal relationships.

Alcohol

Excessive consumption of alcohol may cause these health problems: alcoholism, depression, cirrhosis of the liver, heart failure. Sometimes these problems lead to family breakdown.

Smoking

Smoking can shorten your life by 7 or 8 years. It can also lead to health problems such as: lung cancer (and cancer of other body organs), heart disease, stroke, heart attack.

Drugs

Drugs can become addictive causing serious health problems.

Quick Test

1. How many hours sleep should an adult have?
2. Give two pieces of advice to ensure a good night's sleep.
3. Name three harmful substances which can damage your health.

Answers 1. 6–8 hours. **2.** Do not eat fatty or filling foods before bedtime; relax before going to bed. **3.** Alcohol, cigarettes, drugs if abused.

Consumer advice 1

Sources of advice

Citizens Advice Bureau (CAB)

- This service helps with: debt advice, housing, legal matters, consumer issues, benefits, employment issues, and immigration issues.
- Help can be given with filling out forms, writing letters, negotiating with creditors and representation at court.
- CABs are found in most main towns and cities and online.

Consumer Advice Centre (CAC)

- This agency deals with a wide range of **consumer** problems.
- The trained staff will also introduce you to other sources of help and can assist you with taking action or provide advice on using the Small Claims Court.

Top Tip
Local libraries and school libraries usually have copies of *Which?* magazine.

Consumers' Association (CA)

- The CA provides pre-shopping help and assistance to consumers by carrying out research and full testing of consumer products, from holidays to microwaves. This research is reported in the magazine *Which?*

Consumer Protection Department or Trading Standards Department

- Trading Standards officers enforce a range of laws intended to promote fair trading, consumer protection and environmental safety. Their work ensures that:
  — consumers are not misled by false statements about goods or services
  — consumer goods such as toys and electrical appliances are made to high safety standards.

Environmental Health Department (EHD)

- Environmental Health Officers (EHOs) carry out inspections, enforcement and advisory work in areas of food safety, public health, health and safety in the work place, pollution control and animal welfare.
- EHOs also work with schools and local organisations.

Top Tip
Go to the Leckie & Leckie website to find weblinks for these organisations:
www.leckieandleckie.co.uk/learning_lab

National and Scottish Consumer Council

- These Councils ensure that the interests of all consumers are taken into account by business and industry.
- They do not deal with individual complaints but act as pressure groups nationally.

Consumer rights and responsibilities

A consumer enters into a contract with the seller when they purchase a product. If you have a complaint the seller must remedy (fix) it. A number of laws protect consumers' rights.

The Sale and Supply of Goods Act 1994 (and the Sale and Supply of Goods to Consumers Regulations 2002)

- This Act (and the later Regulations) protect the consumer when buying goods and services in **three** ways, by stating that goods must be: of a **satisfactory quality**, **as described**, and **fit for the purpose**.
- The Act allows consumers a reasonable time to return goods if faulty.
- The Act protects goods bought on sale and second-hand.
- If any of the conditions of the Act are broken, the seller must offer you a full refund, replacement or a credit note.

Top Tip
All goods and services are covered by this Act. Learn the three ways you can be protected by the Act.

Trades Description Act 1968 and 1972

- This Act makes it illegal for traders to falsely describe the goods or services they provide.
- This Act is enforced by the Trading Standards Department.

Consumer Protection Act 1987

This Act protects consumers in two areas:

- Safety: a 'general safety requirement' for domestic goods means that they must be reasonably safe given the likely circumstances in which they will be used.
- Prices: it regulates pricing of goods, services, accommodation or facilities.

Top Tip
Keep records of purchases (receipts or credit card statements) in case you need to return any goods.

Food Safety Act 1990

- This Act ensures that all the food in the food chain is safe to eat. It covers: food premises, food handlers, and food labelling.
- EHOs enforce this Act. They can inspect food or food premises. They have the power to close down a business if there is a health risk to the consumer.

The Food Hygiene (Scotland) Regulations 2006

- All food businesses must carry out a **risk assessment**. All potential food contamination risks have to be identified during the making of their food product.
- Food businesses must take appropriate action to prevent food becoming contaminated
- Equipment and premises involved in food production are kept very clean.
- Food handlers are trained.
- Chilled foods must be kept under refrigeration or a cool ventilated place
- Food being kept hot for sale should be kept at above 63°C
- Reheated food must be raised to at least 82°C

Quick Test

1. Which consumer organisation would provide the best advice for:
   a) a Home Economics Department who wants someone to give a talk on food safety
   b) a consumer who is concerned that the standard of work carried out by a local electrician is not safe.
2. Which Act is enforced by the Trading Standards Department?

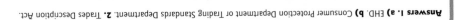

Answers 1. a) EHD. b) Consumer Protection Department or Trading Standards Department. 2. Trades Description Act.

Consumer advice 2

Food labelling

Statutory food labelling

The food label must show the following **statutory** (compulsory) information.

The name of the food or a description of what the product is

- Consumers know exactly what the food is.

A list of ingredients in descending order of weight

- Consumers can see if the product contains ingredients/additives/flavourings they like/dislike, are allergic to, or do not want to eat.

The shelf life showing 'Use by' or 'Best before' dates

- Consumers know when the food should be eaten by, so should only eat 'safe' foods, and therefore reduce the risk of food poisoning. (For more information see page 44.)

Name and address of manufacturer, packer or EU seller

- Needed in case of complaint.
- May encourage consumers to buy particular products.

Weight or volume of product

- Consumers can compare products.
- The **"e"** mark means that the average quantity must be accurate but the weight of each pack may vary slightly.

Country of origin

- Some consumers may not buy products from certain countries for personal or moral reasons.

Storage/Cooking instructions

- If followed correctly, the consumer is assured that food is safe to eat.

Nutritional information

- If a product makes a specific nutritional claim, e.g. low in fat, then this **must** be supported with nutritional information (see page 25).

Top Tip
Keep up to date with labels on food packaging. They give lots of interesting information and will change over time.

Voluntary food labelling

The Seedling symbol shows that the product has been approved by the Vegetarian Society, having met strict criteria. Supermarkets may also have their own symbols.

This symbol shows food has been produced organically, avoiding the routine use of pesticides, antibiotics and other additives and meeting high animal welfare and environmental standards.

Manufacturers of microwave foods include information about heating times depending on the power of the microwave being used.

Other labelling

Gas and electrical equipment

British Gas Seal of Service

This label appears on all gas appliances sold by British Gas. All branded boilers are installed to the highest standards and compliant with relevant appliance specifications.

CORGI (Council for Registered Gas Installers)

This symbol means that the firm is registered with CORGI (a legal requirement) who are satisfied that they are competent gas installers, carry appropriate ID and will work safely within the law.

The British Electrotechnical Approvals Board (BEAB)

This means that BEAB have tested a sample of the product concerned and it meets British Safety Standards.

Double insulation symbol

Products which do not contain an earth should carry this double insulation symbol to show there is lower risk of shock.

The Kitemark

The Kitemark® is a British Standards Institution symbol which shows the product continues to meet high standards of safety, quality and reliability.

Safety and warning labels

This symbol means that the product is toxic and will cause serious harm if swallowed.

Products such as bleach and cleaning products can be very dangerous if not used correctly and so must carry warnings. These symbols show that the product is harmful if swallowed and can cause irritation to the skin.

The Lion Mark

The Lion mark of the British Toy and Hobby Association means that the toy complies with the British Standards (BS EN 71) which ensures the highest standards of safety and quality. Approved Lion Mark Retailers sell only toys which meet the Lion Mark standard.

Upholstered furniture

This means that the material used in upholstered furniture has passed safety tests and is **less likely** to be set alight by matches or cigarettes.

This means that although the filling materials in upholstered furniture passed safety tests, the fabric cover could be set alight by a burning match.

Quick Test

1. List the statutory information which must be found on a food label.

2. What does this symbol mean?

3. What products are given the Lion Mark?

4. Which institution is represented by the Kitemark?

Test your progress

Use the questions to test your progress.

1. List five reasons why we wear clothes. . . . .

2. Give a different reason why the following properties are important for sports clothing.
   a) Absorbency. . . . .
   b) Elasticity. . . . .

3. How does a quilted fabric give warmth to clothing? . . . .

4. List three factors which affect the comfort of a garment. . . . .

5. Which article of children's clothing should have label showing the item is flame resistant? . . . .

6. Why should a baby be dressed in several layers of clothing?. . . . .

7. State two ways in which clothing can be made safer for toddlers. . . . .

8. Elderly people can find fastenings difficult to manage. Give two solutions to this problem. . . . .

9. Which type of home would be most suitable for an elderly couple with mobility problems? Why? . . . .

10. Give two reasons why exercise is important. . . . .

11. Give three areas where the Citizens Advice Bureau can give help. . . . .

12. The Consumers' Association publishes the magazine *Which?* Give two advantages of using the information in *Which?* before purchasing a washing machine. . . . .

13. You have purchased a new tent and on your first outing it has been found to let in the rain.
    a) Name the Act (and year) which protects you in this situation. . . . .

    b) State two ways in which this Act protects the consumer when purchasing goods and services. . . . .

14. State two responsibilities of the Food Safety Act 1990. . . . .

15. Is the following information on food labelling statutory or voluntary?
    a) List of ingredients . . . .
    b) Nutritional information on a 'low fat' product . . . .
    c) Name and address of manufacturer . . . .
    d) Flavourings . . . .

16. What is the name of the symbol which shows that the product meets with the approval of the Vegetarian Society? . . . .

17. What does CORGI stand for? . . . .

18. Which microwave oven would cook faster – 500W or 800W? . . . .

19. What is the name of the symbol for the British Standards Institution? . . . .

How did you do?

1–7 correct	Start again
8–13 correct	Getting there
14–16 correct	Good work
17–19 correct	Excellent

Answers

1. For protection, comfort, safety, to give a particular impression and to give identity.

2. **a)** Absorbency – sportswear which is made from fabric which absorbs moisture/perspiration and then allows that moisture to evaporate helps the wearer feel comfortable; **b)** Elasticity – sportswear which is made from fabric which has elasticity can stretch to allow the wearer to move freely, yet still retain its shape.

3. It ensures good insulation by trapping air.

4. Any 3 answers: size, weight, absorbency, elasticity, softness, crease resistance or fastenings.

5. Nightwear.

6. Because babies find it difficult to control their body temperature and clothing can be added or removed to help maintain body temperature.

7. Any 2 answers: not too long or baggy to prevent falling; no sharp buckles to prevent cuts; no ties or buttons to prevent choking; nightwear should be non-flammable.

8. Velcro fastenings instead of buttons; elastic waistbands or front fastenings which are easier to reach than back fastenings.

9. Any 1 answer: a bungalow – as there are no stairs; a ground floor flat – as there are no stairs.

10. Any 2 answers: makes you feel good; tones the muscles; makes the heart and lungs efficient; aids sleep and appetite; helps use up energy and control weight; helps to reduce stress.

11. Any 3 answers: debt advice, housing, legal matters, consumer issues, benefits, employment and immigration.

12. It will report research into products; it will give test results for products.

13. **a)** Sale and Supply of Goods Act 1990 (Sale and Supply of Goods to Consumers Regulations 2002); **b)** Goods must be: of satisfactory quality, fit for the purpose, and as described.

14. Any 2 answers: food premises; food handlers; food labelling.

15. **a)**, **b)**, **c)**, **d)** Statutory.

16. The Seedling symbol.

17. Confederation of Registered Gas Installers.

18. 800W.

19. The Kitemark.

Income and budgeting

Budgeting priorities

Budgeting is **balancing** the money that comes into the house (**income**) with the money that is spent (**expenditure**).

- If income is **equal to** or **more** than expenditure – this is called a **balanced budget**.

- If expenditure is **more** than income – this is called **debt**.

INCOME   EXPENDITURE

Everyone must budget their money, but we all have different priorities. These depend on:

- amount of income and circumstances: someone who has a limited income (e.g. pensioner, student, single parent) may have to budget more carefully than a professional person who earns a good salary

- the number of people who need to be supported by the income, e.g. parents may have to budget for their child's university education.

There are some things we must spend money on, and other things that are less essential. See pages 78–79 for more about essential and non-essential expenditure.

Main source of income

Income can be classified in two ways:

- **fixed** income – this income remains the same from month to month, e.g. your employment may be paid in a fixed monthly salary

- **variable** income – this income varies from month to month, e.g. sometimes you may be able to earn extra money as overtime.

Top Tip
When planning a budget it is better to rely on **fixed** income rather than **variable** income.

Income source	Explanation
Employment	- Income from employment is usually **fixed**, paid either as a salary (a yearly amount paid in 12 equal monthly payments into your bank account) or as a wage (a fixed rate for each hour worked, which can be paid weekly in cash but is usually paid into a bank account). - Some employment will also pay overtime but this is **variable** income. - Certain deductions will be made from your income before you receive it. These include income tax, national insurance and pension payments.
Pensions	This is a **fixed** payment and can be either a state pension from the government or a private pension.
Benefits	These are **fixed** payments. The government gives money to people who are entitled to receive these payments because they are unemployed, have children, are on low incomes or are too ill or are unable to work.
Interest	Interest is paid on savings or current accounts. The amount will **vary**, depending on how much savings you have.
Dividend	A dividend (similar to interest payments) is paid to people who invest in shares in companies. These payments will also **vary**.

Value for money

Managing money well means getting the best value for the money we spend. We all want 'good deals' so it pays to shop around when buying goods and services.

Buying goods and services

- Compare prices and ranges in various shops, mail order, on the internet and TV shopping.
- Use *Which?* magazine published by the Consumers' Association as this will give you reliable, independent information on a range of products.
- Ask friends, relatives or shop assistants for advice, but remember, this may be biased information.

Top Tip
Free delivery is offered by some stores. Internet shopping can save time.

Shopping for food

- Buying non-perishable goods in bulk from a cash and carry or supermarket may be cheaper, providing you have sufficient storage space.
- Take advantage of special offers such as money-off coupons.
- Perishable food (e.g. bread) is often reduced at the end of the shopping day.
- Supermarkets' own brands are often cheaper than 'brand' names.
- Discount supermarkets are often cheaper than mainstream supermarkets but may stock less well-known brands.

Top Tip
Supermarkets have a wide range of goods but remember small local shops, although usually more expensive than supermarkets, may have special offers and give a more personal service.

Shopping for credit

- Check the rate of interest which will be charged. This is called the Annual Percentage Rate (APR). The higher the APR then the more expensive the credit will be if you don't pay the full amount owed each month.
- Check the deposit required and the period of repayment.
- Check which credit lender will give you the best deal.
- Think about how much you can afford, bearing in mind your fixed income.

Quick Test

1. Why is it important to balance the household budget?

2. List two sources of income which can vary.

3. What does APR stand for?

4. List three sources of advice you could use before deciding which cooker to buy.

Answers 1. To avoid debt. **2.** Overtime; interest; dividend. **3.** Annual percentage rate. **4.** Friends; relatives; shop assistants; *Which?* magazine; internet.

Essential and non-essential expenditure

Expenditure can be classified as:

- **essential**: spending on things you **need** and **must pay for** to survive
- **non-essential**: spending on things you **could do without**.

Anything that is bought must be paid for, eventually. The key is to work out what **needs** to be bought, **how much** can be spent, and **how** it should be paid for.

Top Tip
All household expenditure will vary depending on income, the size and composition of the family, and the family's spending priorities.

Essential expenditure

Food

Food is an essential purchase, and having a balanced diet is important to good health. You can economise on food expenditure by shopping around.

Clothing

Clothes help keep us warm and protect us from the weather, but some are more essential than others, e.g. school uniforms and warm clothing for winter are more important than 'fashion' items. Spending on essential clothing should be given priority over non-essential items.

Shelter

Unless the home is fully paid for, money must be spent on rent or mortgage. This is an important priority as you could lose your home if these payments are not met.

Maintenance of shelter

This area includes general maintenance costs, cleaning and repairs to the house. Repairs should be carried out sooner rather than later to prevent further damage.

Fuel

Gas and electricity costs cover heating, lighting and cooking. Fuel bills vary throughout the year, e.g. in winter heating bills usually rise due to cold weather.

Taxes/Insurances

Income tax and National Insurance are deducted from your pay but you have to budget for Council tax. You can take out insurance policies on belongings (house and contents, car, etc.) and on health.

Debit and credit arrangements

These payments must be made regularly (usually monthly). If you do not pay the amount owing in full, interest will be added each month, increasing the overall amount owed. If you are unable to make regular payments, the goods can be taken from you and you could be prosecuted for non-payment.

Non-essential expenditure

Non-essential expenditure will vary according to the amount of income available and the spending priorities of the household. Priorities will vary according to the age, interests, values and beliefs of different family members. For example, a single person with a very stressful job may consider a holiday to be essential part of their budget, whereas a family with teenage children may consider membership of sports and leisure clubs to be important.

Top Tip
If a budget becomes overspent then it is the non-essential areas where savings could be made first.

Transport

This could be considered essential or non-essential. If you have to use transport to get to and from work then it is essential. If you could walk or cycle to work then savings could be made in this area if the cost of transport is a problem. The cost of owning, using and maintaining a car also comes into this area.

Personal purchases

This includes a variety of items which could be considered as luxuries, e.g. perfume, cosmetics, aftershave, books, magazines, CDs. This is one area where savings can be made.

Savings

If you have sufficient income, it is good idea to try to save some money for emergencies, gifts, holidays, clothes, etc.

Entertainment/Sport/Leisure

This includes cinema visits, nightclubs, football matches, ice skating, membership of sports clubs, etc. This is an area where considerable savings can often be made.

Travel and holidays

Holidays need not be expensive. But extra money is often needed for travel insurance, spending while on holiday, and new purchases needed for the holiday (e.g. tent for camping, clothes for skiing).

Top Tip
In the exam a question on budgeting may relate to a case study. Underline the key information given in the case study as this will affect the budgeting priorities you need to describe.

Quick Test

1. What are the two types of expenditure?
2. What factors will affect the amount of money spent on clothes in a family?
3. Give one reason why payment for debit and credit agreements should be met.

Answers 1. Essential and non-essential. **2.** Amount of income available: age, sex and interests of family members. **3.** To avoid the goods being removed, debt or prosecution.

Purchasing goods

Methods of payment

The range of payment methods available to consumers depends on their financial circumstances and lifestyle, as well as the type of goods to be purchased.

Some people prefer to pay for their goods more or less **immediately** by the following methods.

Method of payment	Main points
Cash	This method prevents debt as you can only buy goods to the value of the money you have with you.
Electronic Funds Transfer at Point of Sale (EFTPOS), e.g. Switch cards	The customer receives a plastic debit card (a cash card). When buying goods, the card is swiped through the till and the amount of money spent is instantly debited (taken) from the bank account.
Personal cheques and cheque card	Customers are provided with a cheque book and cheque card. The cheque card guarantees to the shop keeper that the cheque will be honoured (paid for) up to the amount stated on the card. You must be careful not to write cheques that total more than the amount of money in your bank account, or they will 'bounce'.
Credit card, e.g. Visa, Mastercard	The customer is given a plastic card and a specified credit limit. The card is swiped through the till at purchase. A monthly statement shows the amount of money spent during that month. This amount (the balance) can be paid **in full** or **in part**. If you do not pay all the balance, then interest will be added to the remaining (outstanding) balance.
Charge card, e.g. American Express	This is similar to a credit card – the difference is that **the balance must be paid in full** at the end of the month. A fee is charged annually for administration costs.

Some people prefer to **defer** payments on the goods they buy ('buy now, pay later'). This allows them to pay for the goods over a longer period of time. Distributing payments over time may make budgeting easier, but interest may increase the final cost.

Method of payment	Main points
Credit sale	An initial deposit is paid and the balance paid over several months in fixed payments. You own the goods straight away so these cannot be taken away from you but you can be prosecuted for non-payment if you fail to make the agreed payments.
Hire purchase	An initial deposit is paid with the balance being paid over several months in fixed payments – interest is usually charged. With hire purchase, although you can take the goods with you, you **do not own** them until all the payments have been made. The goods can be taken away if payments are not kept up.

Top Tip

You must consider the financial situation of the target group identified in the exam question to ensure the most suitable method of payment is chosen.

Store budget account	This works like a credit card but its use is limited to certain stores or groups of stores. Customers are given a credit limit and regular payments have to be made each month. Interest charges can be high.
Store charge account	This works like a credit card but can only be used in certain stores. Interest charges can be high.

Top Tip
If buying goods on credit, always maintain regular payments as credit companies check on your credit history. If you have had debt problems in the past you may not be allowed credit in the future.

Paying by cash

Advantages
- Easy and convenient way to pay for items.
- Less risk of debt as you can only buy what you can afford.

Disadvantages
- Money can be lost or stolen.
- You can lose out on genuine bargains or temporary special offers.

Paying by credit

Top Tip
You have to be over 18 to obtain credit.

Advantages
- You don't need to carry large amounts of cash around.
- You can take advantage of bargains.
- If the goods cost more than £100 and are faulty and the shop you purchased them from has closed down then you can make a claim from the credit card provider.
- Credit and charge cards can be used to obtain money from a cash machine.

Disadvantages
- You may have to pay interest so cost of item increases.
- It is easy to overspend and run up debts.
- Credit and store cards can be lost or stolen so increasing the risk of fraud.
- You could forget your personal identification number (PIN) and not be able to use the card.

Quick Test

1. What is the advantage of paying for goods by the deferred payment system?
2. State one disadvantage of paying for goods by cash.
3. List two factors which affect the method of payment chosen by consumers.
4. If you only pay some of the outstanding balance of your credit card, what will happen?

Answers 1. Allows cost to be spread over a period of time; may help budgeting. **2.** Money can be lost; money can be stolen; may not be able to take advantage of bargains. **3.** Financial circumstances; type of lifestyle; type of goods. **4.** You will be charged interest on the outstanding balance.

Debt management

Procedure to follow if debt occurs

It is very easy to get into debt if you do not watch your spending carefully. Avoid debt by keeping a record of **all** weekly or monthly expenditure and make sure it is less than your income. If you are spending too much, then you should first look at your expenditure on **non-essential** items and see if you can cut back in some areas.

If you get into serious debt then more serious action has to be taken. What steps can you take to help get out of debt?

Step	Explanation
Do not ignore the problem. Do not ignore letters and phone calls from your creditors (the people who you owe money to).	The debt will not go away so you should seek help. Your creditors may be able to provide support (after all, they want you to be able to pay the money back).
Do not take on any further debt; do not borrow any further money to pay off your debts.	This will only make the situation worse and the debt may increase.
Look carefully at your budget. Make detailed, accurate notes of your monthly income and expenditure.	This will help you see where money is spent and in what areas you can cut back, e.g. non-essential spending. Your creditor may request this information before they can assist you.
Tackle priority debts first.	These are debts relating to essential items, e.g. mortgage or the gas/electricity bill. Non-payment of these can mean losing your home or having the fuel cut off.
Contact all creditors immediately and explain your current financial difficulties.	This helps creditors become aware of your problem – they may come up with a plan to help you, such as extending the repayment time or reducing the monthly repayments.
Keep a record of all telephone calls, correspondence and repayments.	This will help you see how you are managing to cope with the debt and encourage you to keep going until all the debt is paid off.
Cut up or destroy all credit cards.	This reduces the temptation to spend and get into more debt.
Contact agencies which can help you. (See page 83.)	You may find it useful (and less embarrassing) to speak to someone who does not know you personally. You will be given helpful and practical advice on your debt problem.

Sources of advice

There are a number of different agencies that can give you advice about debt problems.

Citizens Advice Bureau (CAB)

- These are found in most main towns and cities and some provide an online service.
- The advice given is free, independent and confidential.
- Advisers have been trained and will help to come up with a debt management plan based on what you can afford.
- They can also help negotiate with creditors.

Consumer Advice Centre (CAC)

- The advice given is free, independent and confidential.
- Staff are trained to give advice on debt management.

Company/bank/building society concerned

- If money is owed to any of these organisations, most will be willing to help you solve your debt problems by offering free advice, but first you have to make them aware of the problem.
- Some companies advertise in the media and offer a package to help you reduce your monthly credit payments by dealing with your creditors.
- You may be charged a monthly fee for this service, which could be better used to pay off your original debt.
- The Consumer Credit Counselling Service (CCCS) will carry out a similar service at no charge.

Credit Union

- Credit Unions are set up in local communities to offer local people financial services.
- Trained staff will give advice on money management; they may give the advice themselves or they will refer you to another organisation, e.g. CAB, for further help.

Quick Test

1. If you are in debt, why should you not borrow any more money?

2. If you are in debt, why should you cut up or destroy all your credit cards?

3. List four agencies that could help with debt management.

Answers 1. This will only make the situation worse and the debt may increase. **2.** This reduces the temptation to spend and get into more debt. **3.** Citizens Advice Bureau; Consumer Advice Centre; Credit Union; Company/bank/building society concerned.

Test your progress

Use the questions to test your progress.

1. Explain the term 'balanced budget'. . . . .

2. Explain the difference between fixed income and variable income. . . . .

3. Apart from employment, state two other sources of fixed income. . . . .

4. Explain the difference between essential and non-essential expenditure. . . . .

5. Why is shelter an essential area of expenditure? . . . .

6. What factors will affect the amount of money spent on food? . . . .

7. State two non-essential areas of expenditure where savings could be made. . . . .

8. What must you be sure of before you write any cheques? . . . .

9. Explain the difference between a charge card and a credit card. . . . .

10. Explain the difference between hire purchase and a credit sale agreement. . . . .

11. What is the minimum age to obtain credit? . . . .

12. Give two advantages of buying goods on credit. . . . .

13. Give two disadvantages of buying goods on credit. . . . .

14. **a)** Give an advantage of using information in the Consumers' Association magazine *Which?* before purchasing a washing machine. . . . .

    b) State two other sources of information which could be used before buying the washing machine to ensure best value for money. . . . .

15. List two pieces of advice you could give a student living on her own and on a limited budget to ensure best value for money when shopping for food. . . . .

16. Give two different pieces of advice you could give a family of two adults and three children to ensure best value for money when shopping for food. . . . .

17. List two points to consider when shopping for credit to ensure best value for money. . . . .

18. List three steps you could take to prevent debt from getting further out of control. . . . .

19. How can the Citizens Advice Bureau help with debt problems? . . . .

Answers

1. A balanced budget is one where the money that comes into the house (income) is more than or equal to the money that is spent (expenditure).

2. Fixed income – income will remain the same from month to month, e.g. your employment may be paid in a fixed monthly salary; Variable income – income will vary from month to month, e.g. overtime.

3. Pensions, benefits.

4. Essential – a type of expenditure that must be paid; non-essential – a type of expenditure that you could do without.

5. You could lose your home if required payments are not met.

6. The size and composition of the family.

7. Any 2 answers: transport, personal purchases, entertainment/sport/leisure, travel and holidays.

8. That there is sufficient money in the bank account to cover the cheques.

9. A charge card must be paid in full each month; a credit card can be paid in part.

10. With a credit sale agreement you own the goods straight away so these cannot be taken away from you but you can be prosecuted for non-payment; with hire purchase you do not own the goods until all the payments have been made, so the goods can be taken away if payments are not kept up.

11. 18 years.

12. Any 2 answers: saves having to carry large amounts of cash around; can take advantage of bargains, e.g. at sale times and spread the cost over a period of time; if the goods cost more than £100 and are faulty and the shop you purchased them from has closed down then you can make a claim from the credit card provider.

13. Any 2 answers: you may have to pay interest so cost of item increases; it is easy to overspend and run up debts; credit and store cards can be lost or stolen so increasing the risk of fraud; you might forget your PIN.

14. **a)** It gives you reliable, independent information on a range of products.
    b) Any 2 answers: shops, mail order, internet, TV shopping, friends/relatives, shop assistants.

15. Any 2 answers: take advantage of special offers, money-off coupons; some food (e.g. bread) is often reduced at the end of the shopping day; supermarkets' own brands can often be cheaper; discount supermarkets are often cheaper but will stock less well known brands.

16. Any 2 answers (but must be different from answers given to previous question): buying in bulk from a cash and carry or supermarket may be cheaper providing you have sufficient storage space; take advantage of special offers, money-off coupons; some food (e.g. bread) is often reduced at the end of the shopping day; supermarkets' own brands can often be cheaper; discount supermarkets are often cheaper but will stock less well known brands; free delivery is offered by some stores and internet food ordering can be time saving.

17. Any 2 answers: check the rate of interest (APR) which will be charged; check the deposit required and the period of repayment; check which credit lender will give you the best deal; think about how much you can afford – bear in mind your fixed income.

18. Any 3 answers: do not ignore the problem; do not ignore letters and phone calls from your creditors; do not take on any further debt – do not borrow any further money to pay off your debts; look carefully at your budget; make detailed, accurate notes of your monthly income and expenditure; tackle priority debts first; contact all the creditors immediately and explain your current financial difficulties; keep a record of all telephone calls, correspondence and repayments; cut up or destroy all credit cards; contact agencies which can help you.

19. Trained advisers will help to come up with a debt management plan based on what you can afford; they can also help negotiate with creditors.

Questions

Question 1 – General KU

Two 13 year old boys are hungry and have decided to make a snack before they go to football practice. The snack is a wholemeal toast sandwich with grated cheese served with a mixed salad.

a) Choose a **different main** nutrient found in each of the foods. [3]

b) Complete the nutrition table below. [3]

Food	Nutrient	Function of nutrient in the body
Wholemeal toast		
Cheese		
Mixed salad		

Question 2 – Credit KU CREDIT

a) Explain the importance of the interrelationship between iron and vitamin C. [1]

b) Explain the function of calcium in the diet. [1]

Question 3 – General KU

Grilling and steaming are two healthy methods of cooking food.

Choose **one** method and explain why it is healthy. [2]

Question 4 – Credit KU CREDIT

Identify and explain **three** factors related to an individual's diet which may contribute to coronary heart disease. [6]

Question 5 – General KU

The choice of food made by an individual is affected by a number of factors.

a) Identify **two** factors that affect food choice. [2]

b) Explain why **each** affects food choice. [2]

Question 6 – Credit KU CREDIT

Identify and explain **two** diet-related health problems common to elderly people. [4]

Question 7 – Credit HI CREDIT

A 55 year old man is a member of the local mountain rescue team. His father and grandfather both had heart disease. He takes a packed lunch to mountain rescue practices.

a) Taking account of the Dietary Reference Values for Males aged 50+ years and the contribution that lunch should make to his daily requirements, **evaluate the suitability** of his packed lunch. [9]

Dietary Reference Values for Males aged 50+ years

Estimated Average Requirement	Reference Nutrient Intakes				
	Protein	Iron	Vitamin A	Vitamin B2	Sodium
Energy					
10.60 MJ	53.3g	8.7mg	700mg	1.3mg	1600mg
Lunch should provide approximately ¹/₃ of day's requirements					
	Protein	Iron	Vitamin A	Vitamin B2	Sodium
Energy					
3.53 MJ	17.8g	2.9mg	233mg	0.4mg	533mg

Dietary Analysis of Packed Lunch

Energy	Protein	Iron	Vitamin A	Vitamin B2	Sodium
4.43 MJ	12.2g	1.4mg	274mg	0.9mg	440mg

b) The man has made an egg mayonnaise sandwich as part of the packed lunch. He will be involved with rescue practice for four hours before eating his lunch. Identify and explain **two** factors related to bacterial growth which could make the sandwich a food safety risk. **[4]**

Question 8 – General KU

The following care label appears on a jacket.

A   B   C   D ○

Choose **two** symbols from this label.

a) Explain the meaning of **each** symbol. **[2]**

b) Give a reason why **each** symbol would make this jacket a good choice for a teenager. **[2]**

Question 9 – General KU

A family is planning a birthday party for their 5-year-old child and his very lively friends. It is very important that the house is safe for these children.

Look at the following picture of the living room.

Identify **three** ways the room could be made safer for the children. **[3]**

Explain why **each** change would make the room safer for the children. **[3]**

Question 10 – General HI

Read the information about the Smith family.

> Mr and Mrs Smith have two teenage children. Both parents are employed. The family shop is done once a week. They are going to buy a new fridge freezer. The floor space available for this is 60cm width (W) x 65cm depth (D). The family try to be as energy-efficient as possible.

Study the information below on four different models they are considering.

Features	Model A	Model B	Model C	Model D
Cost	£226	£199	£300	£299
Dimensions (cm²)	60W x 66D	54W x 56.5D	60W x 65D	60W x 65.5D
Automatic fridge defrost	Yes	Yes	Yes	No
Automatic freezer defrost	Yes	Yes	Yes	No
Volume of food which can be stored in fridge (litres)	183.0	155.0	201.0	230.0
Volume of food which can be stored in freezer (litres)	113.0	105.0	115.0	100.0
Energy rating	B	A	A	A

a) Choose the **most** suitable model for the family [1]

b) Give **two different** reasons for your choice [4]

Question 11 – Credit KU

A primary school child who walks to school has a new winter jacket. The jacket has the following design features:

- quilted padding
- reflective strips
- elasticated cuffs

Choose **two** design features and give **different** reasons why each one is important. [4]

Question 12 – Credit HI

Study the information below about shoes for a young child.

Shoes A

- Soft leather uppers
- Flexible non-slip sole
- Smooth leather lining
- Heel and arch support
- Padded ankle support
- Colour choice; navy or lilac
- Available in infant sizes: 6, 6¹/₂, 7, 7¹/₂, 8, 8¹/₂, 9, 9¹/₂, 10
- 3 width fittings

Shoes B

- Man-made fabric upper
- Smooth rigid sole
- Man-made lining
- Cushioned ankle support
- Contrast stitched trim
- Colour choice: black or brown
- Available in infant sizes: 6, 7, 8, 9, 10

a) Which shoes are **more** suitable for a young child who is learning how to walk? [1]

b) Give **two different** reasons for your choice. [4]

Question 13 – General HI

Ann is a 15 year old school girl who has decided to join a step aerobic class.
She has a choice of two outfits to wear.

Study the information below on her two choices.

Outfit	Fibre	Elasticity	Ease of washing	Absorbency	Durability	Weight
A T shirt	Cotton	****	*****	*****	*****	Light
Shorts	Lycra	*****	***	***	*****	Light
B Sweatshirt	Cotton	***	*****	*****	*****	Medium
Jogging trousers	Polyester	***	***	**	*****	Medium

Key: Good ***** ⟶ Poor *

a) Which outfit is **more** suitable for Ann to wear to the step aerobic class? [1]

b) Give **two** reasons for your choice. [4]

Question 14 – Credit KU

Explain, in detail, **two different** reasons why exercise makes an important contribution to maintaining a healthy lifestyle for a teenager. [4]

Question 15 – General KU

Mr and Mrs Black, a retired elderly couple on a pension, are planning to buy a new washing machine. The model they are considering costs £269.99.

Choose **one** of the following methods and explain **one** advantage and **one** disadvantage of paying by this method. [4]

- cash
- credit card

Answers

Note: Sample answers provided here vary in depth and range, reflecting the variable nature of likely responses and providing support where students traditionally experience difficulty in giving answers of sufficient detail to gain full marks.

Question 1 – General KU

a) 3 x 1 mark for correctly linking nutrient to food [3]

b) 3 x 1 mark for identifying function of each nutrient [3]

Nutrient	Food	Function of nutrient in the body
Carbohydrate	Wholemeal toast/ Mixed salad	Used as a source of energy and warmth Filling, so less likely to snack on high fat/sugar foods Used as source of NSP
Fat	Cheese	Used for warmth and energy Provides fat soluble vitamins A and D Provides essential fatty acids
Protein	Cheese/Wholemeal toast	Used for growth, repair and maintenance of body tissues Used as a secondary source of energy
Vitamin C	Mixed salad	Assists in the absorption of iron Helps prevent anaemia Required to make connective tissue Helps cuts and wounds to heal more quickly Is an antioxidant vitamin
Vitamin A	Mixed salad	Assists with the development of good vision particularly in dim light Is an antioxidant vitamin Aids normal growth in children
Calcium	Cheese/Wholemeal toast	Helps with the formation and maintenance of strong bones and teeth Helps prevent rickets/brittle bones/osteoporosis
Iron	Wholemeal toast	Needed to form haemoglobin Carries oxygen round the body Helps prevent anaemia

Question 2 – Credit KU

a) 1 mark for any one of the following answers [1]

- The absorption of iron is increased by the presence of vitamin C and so prevents anaemia
- If there is not enough vitamin C the body may be unable to absorb the iron, so there will be less haemoglobin to carry the oxygen to the cells and so tiredness may result
- The body requires vitamin C to aid the absorption of iron, especially important for females when they are menstruating, so this will help prevent anaemia

b) 1 mark [1]

Sample answer (check page 12 for other possible answers):

- Calcium helps develop strong bones and teeth; if it is lacking in the diet then it could cause rickets/softening of bones/poor bone development in children/osteoporosis in adults

Question 3 – General KU [2]

2 x 1 mark for each answer for either method; reasons must be different

Grilling
- No fat is added to the food/food may be lightly brushed during this method of cooking
- Some fat drains away so fat content is reduced
- Fewer water soluble vitamins are lost

Steaming
- No fat is added to the food during cooking so there is less fat
- The food does not come into direct contact with water, so loss of water soluble vitamins/vitamin C/vitamin B is limited

Question 4 – Credit KU [6]

3 x 1 mark for each factor; 3 x 1 mark for each explanation

Sample answer (check page 23 for other possible answers):

High intake of:
- saturated/animal fats/example of fatty foods
  These contain cholesterol which builds up in the blood and is deposited on walls of arteries, causing arteries to narrow which may lead to heart disease/increased risk of blood clots/heart attacks.
- salt/sodium/example of salty foods
  This causes high blood pressure which may lead to heart disease.

Low intake of:
- NSP/fruit and vegetables/ wholegrain foods
  The diet may be low in NSP which helps reduce the amount of cholesterol in the blood, and so a low intake increases the risk of heart disease.

Question 5 – General KU [4]

2 x 1 mark for each factor; 2 x 1 mark for each explanation

Sample answer (check page 33 for other possible answers):

Available income
- The amount of income will affect the quality and type of food purchased. A low income may mean less fruit and vegetables but more fatty and sugary foods are purchased. However, a high income does not necessarily mean that a more healthy diet will be eaten.

Advertising
- Access to advertising may affect food choice, e.g. may encourage a poor choice or raise awareness of new choices.

Question 6 – Credit KU [4]

2 x 1 mark for each health problem; 2 x 1 mark for each explanation

Sample answer (check page 30 for other possible answers):

Osteomalacia
- A shortage of calcium/vitamin D foods in the diet will result in poor absorption of calcium, so bones can become brittle and easily broken.

Anaemia
- The elderly person may not eat sufficient sources of iron-rich foods such as red meat/may eat a lot of snacks instead of a balanced diet, so anaemia may develop.

Question 7 – Credit HI CREDIT

a) 3 x 1 mark for evaluating the suitability of the nutrient or energy intake   **[3]**

3 x 1 mark for explaining the importance of the nutrient or energy intake linked to the situation/case study   **[3]**

3 x 1 mark for stating the consequence to the situation/case study   **[3]**

Evaluating suitability	Importance	Consequences
Energy The energy intake is higher than the EAR which is acceptable *Or* The energy intake is too high which is not good	As he could be quite active and so use energy as part of the rescue team As he may not use up a lot of energy apart from the rescue team	So he will be provided with sufficient energy for the rescue activities and so will not feel tired/concentration on task will be maintained So he may become obese if he consistently overeats the rest of the day which will contribute to the risk of heart disease
Protein The packed lunch is lower/almost 1/3 lower than the RNI which is not good	As protein could be needed to repair any damaged tissues as a result of being in the mountain rescue team	So cuts and wounds may be less likely to repair as well if the protein intake is continually low
Iron The packed lunch contains less iron than RNI/half the amount required which is not good	As iron is required to make haemoglobin/red cells which carry oxygen round the body	So this will result in his feeling tired and listless and possibly developing anaemia
Vitamin A Has more than the RNI which is good	As vitamin A helps vision in dim light *Or* As vitamin A is an antioxidant vitamin	So his eyesight will manage to adapt if called out on a night rescue So a good supply of antioxidant vitamins will help reduce his risk of heart disease
Vitamin B2 Is more than double the RNI which is good	As vitamin B2 releases energy from food	So he will be provided with the energy to carry out rescue activities
Sodium Sodium intake is satisfactory as it is below the RNI *Or* Sodium intake is below RNI which could be a problem long term	As sodium maintains correct blood pressure As sodium is required for correct muscle function	So less sodium reduces the man's risk of high blood pressure, especially as he has an added risk of heart disease So he could suffer from cramp in his legs when on mountain rescue activities

b) 2 x 1 mark for each factor; 2 x 1 mark for each explanation   **[4]**

Sample answer (check pages 40–41 for other possible answers):

Temperature

- Bacteria multiply quickly in warm temperatures which could lead to food poisoning from the sandwich filling.

Food

- Mayonnaise is a high risk food, ideal for the multiplication of bacteria.

Question 8 – General KU

2 x 1 mark for each meaning; 2 x 1 mark for each reason   **[4]**

A Can be machine washed at 40°C with minimal action

- Machine washing is quick and easy and the teenager may wear the jacket often
- Teenager may not want or have time to hand wash

B Do not iron
- Teenager may not enjoy/have time for ironing especially if jacket is washed and worn frequently

C Can be tumble dried
- Jacket can be quickly dried after washing – handy if jacket is worn frequently

D Do not dry clean
- Dry cleaning would be expensive for a teenager

Question 9 – General KU

3 x 1 mark for each safe way; 3 x 1 extra mark (+) for relating the way to the needs of the children **[6]**

Ways to make room safer	Relating to needs of children
The fire should have a fireguard	+ so that the children cannot accidentally fall in when playing and be burnt
The TV flex should be shortened/routed round the edge of the room/plugged in to a nearer socket/removed from the socket while the children are there	+ the children could trip and fall over the flex while playing
The matches should be stored safely away before the party starts	+ as a child could play with them and be burnt/others may be burnt/cause a house fire
The sharp knife should be stored away safely before the party starts	+ the children may pick up the knife and cut themselves or others
Pills should be locked away	+ the children may think they are sweets and could be poisoned if they swallow the pills
The electric socket should have a safety cover on it	+ to prevent the children sticking their fingers/sharp objects into it and being electrocuted

Question 10 – General HI

a) Model C **[1]**

b) 2 x 1 mark for linking table to case study; 2 x 1 extra mark (+) for relating reason to the needs of the Smiths **[4]**

Feature	Reason	Why reason relates to Smith family
Cost	It is the most expensive fridge/freezer but both parents work	+ and it would be worth the money as it has other desirable features for the family
Dimensions	It will fit into the space in the Smith's kitchen	+ as the kitchen is fitted no changes could be made to layout
Automatic fridge defrost and freezer defrost	This means that no time/effort will have to be spent defrosting the equipment	+ important as both parents work so do not have the time
Volume of food in refrigerator	Can store a good volume of food in the fridge section – second highest	+ important as there are four people in the family so there will be a good quantity of food requiring storage + the shopping is only done once a week so there will be a quantity of food requiring storage
Volume of food in freezer	Can store the largest volume of frozen food of all the fridge/freezers	+ additional marks as for refrigerator
Energy ratings	Has an A for energy rating which is the best	+ important as the family want to save energy and this fridge freezer will do this due to its rating

Exam-style questions and answers

Question 11 – Credit KU

2 x 1 mark for explaining usefulness of design feature; 2 x 1 extra mark (+) for relating explanation to child **[4]**

Quilted padding
- May be required for warmth + as the child walks to and from school on cold days

Reflective strips
- Required for safety + as the child must be visible when walking to/from school on dark winter days; or
  + so that cars can see the child in the dark/prevent accidents

Elasticated cuffs
- To help keep the child warm + to prevent rain/snow from getting up the sleeves when walking to school

Question 12 – Credit HI

a) Shoes A **[1]**

b) 2 x 1 mark for correctly linking table to child; 2 x 1 extra mark (+) for relating the reason to the child learning to walk **[4]**

Feature	Relating to child	Relating to learning to walk
Soft leather uppers	Will be comfortable to wear as they are flexible	+ will not damage foot when learning to walk
Flexible non-slip sole	Will bend with the foot when walking and provide secure grip	+ will make it easier to take steps + less chance of slipping when learning to walk so safer
Smooth leather lining	Will protect the feet from hard seams or stitching	+ will prevent soreness when walking
Heel and arch support	Gives support where it is needed when learning to walk	+ important to keep the foot in good shape
Padded ankle support	Gives support around the ankle Gives a snug fit, preventing the shoe slipping up and down	+ important when a child is unsteady on feet + so prevents rubbing and friction when walking
Colour choice: navy or lilac	Although will not affect walking a colour choice may encourage child to practise walking/a suitable colour available for boys and girls	+ lilac colour may be brighter for summer/may appeal to child more
Available in infant half sizes from 6 to 10	Half sizes will allow for proper fitting of shoe/room for toes	+ important for growth when learning to walk
3 width fittings	Width fitting will allow for proper fitting of shoe	+ important to give good support when learning to walk

Question 13 – General HI

a) Outfit A **[1]**

b) 2 x 1 mark for correctly linking table to the case study; 2 x 1 extra mark (+) for relating the reason to the needs of Ann **[4]**

Property	Feature of property	Why suitable for Ann's needs
Elasticity	Elasticity is needed because it allows movement when exercising	+ this will allow Ann to move easily in class
Ease of washing	T shirt has a good rating and the shorts have an average rating, making it easy for Ann to wash the outfit	+ as the outfit will need to be washed after every class due to perspiration when exercising

Absorbency	The T shirt will absorb the perspiration during the class	+ this will make Ann feel more comfortable
Durability	A good rating shows the outfit will last for some time	+ outfit can withstand the movements involved in step aerobics
Weight	The light weight of both T shirt and shorts means they will be comfortable to wear when taking part in the class	+ and will not restrict movement through being too heavy

Question 14 – Credit KU

2 x 1 mark for correct reason; 2 x 1 extra mark (+) for relating the reason to teenagers **[4]**

- Gives a feeling of well-being, reduces stress
  + and so raises the self esteem of the teenager/teenager becomes more alert and focused
- Makes heart work more efficiently/organs function better
  + encourages future good health for the teenager/less risk of heart disease
- Helps lose/maintain weight
  + prevents the risk of teenager becoming obese
- Helps to develop strong bones
  + reduces the risk of osteoporosis for the teenager in later life
- Promotes restful sleep
  + will improve overall standard of teenager's learning ability/work/performance in all areas of life/teenager becomes more alert and focused

Question 15 – General KU

2 x 1 mark for correct explanation of advantage/disadvantage; 2 x 1 extra mark (+) for relating the reason to the Blacks' needs **[4]**

Cash – *Advantages*

- Easy and convenient way to pay for items
  + pensioners often don't like the idea of debt
- Less risk of debt as they can only buy what they can afford
  + as pensioners they may be on a limited budget
- May get a discount if paying by cash
  + so may be able to use the money saved on essential bills, e.g. heating as elderly may feel the cold

Cash – *Disadvantages*

- Not very safe to carry large amounts of cash around
  + pensioners are a vulnerable group
- Money can be lost
  + pensioners cannot afford to lose money if on a limited budget

Credit card – *Advantages*

- Saves having to carry large amounts of cash around with them
  + so it is safer/more convenient/eliminates the loss of money for the pensioners
- Spreads the cost over a period of time
  + so assists with budgeting especially if on a limited income
- If the goods cost more than £100 and are faulty and the shop they purchased from has closed down then they can make a claim to the credit card provider
  + added consumer protection for the couple
- May have the opportunity for interest free credit
  + saves money if on a limited income

Credit card – *Disadvantages*

- May have to pay interest
  + so cost of item increases for them, difficult if on a limited budget
- Credit and store cards can be lost or stolen
  + so increasing the risk of fraud/lost money for pensioners

Index

accommodation 68
adolescents 29, 66
adults 30
amino acids 8
anaemia 22

babies/toddlers 66
bacteria 38–39, 42
biological value 8
bowel disorders 22
bread 18, 20
breastfeeding 28, 33
budgeting 76–79

calcium 12, 15
cancer 22
carbohydrates 8–9, 20
cereals 18, 20
children 29, 66
chutney making 41
Citizens Advice Bureau
    (CAB) 70, 83
clothing 64–67
conservation (resources) 60
constipation 22
consumer advice 70–73, 83
Consumers' Association (CA) 70
contamination (food) 42
cooking methods 19
coronary heart disease (CHD) 23
costs (reducing) 60–61
credit 81, 83

date marking 44
debt 82–83
design (product) 57–61
dietary
    reference values (DRVs) 28
    requirements 28–32
    targets 18, 20–21
diverticular disease 22

elderly 30, 67
energy 60–61
Environmental Health Department
    (EHD) 70
equipment (choice) 56–57
essential
    amino acids 8
    fatty acids (EFA) 9
estimated average requirements

(EAR) 28
exams 4-7
    questions/answers 86–95
expenditure 78–79

fat 9, 18, 19, 21
    soluble vitamins 10
fibre (dietary) 13, 22–24, 28–29
fish 18, 20
fluoride 12
folic acid 11
food
    buying 43
    choices 33
    hygiene 37
    labelling 25, 44, 72
    poisoning 40
    preparation 48
    preserving 41
    spoilage 38–39
    storing 43–44
    transporting 43
freezers 41, 45
fruit 18, 20

haemorrhoids 22
handling information (HI) 6-7
hazards 52-53
health (and nutrients) 14–15,
    28–32
heart disease 23
home safety 52–53
hygiene
    food 37
    personal 36–37
hypertension 23

income 76
infants (diet) 28
insulation 60
iron 12, 15

jam making 41

kitchen hygiene 37
knowledge and understanding
    (KU) 4–5

labelling 25, 44, 72
lactovegetarian 32
laws (consumer) 71

marmalade making 41
minerals 12
moulds 38

nutrients 8–12, 14–15, 28–32

obesity 24
osteomalacia 30
osteoporosis 30

payment methods 80–81
personal hygiene 36
pH level 40
phosphorus 15
pickling 41
pregnancy 31, 67
preserving (food) 41
product design 57–59
proteins 8
purchasing goods 80

recycling 61
reference nutrient intake (RNI) 28
refrigerators 45
resources (conservation) 60–61

safe practices 48–53
    labelling 73
salt 18, 20
sewing 51
shelter 68
sodium 12
stroke 23
sugar 18, 21

tooth decay 23

vacuum packaging 41
value for money 77
vegan 32
vegetables 18, 20
vegetarian 32
vitamins 10–11, 15

washing (clothes) 36
water 13
    soluble vitamins 10–11
weight control 24
well-being 69

yeasts 38